CW00664262

RITUAL

ALSO BY DAMIEN ECHOLS ✕ LORRI DAVIS

Yours for Eternity

ALSO BY DAMIEN ECHOLS

Life After Death

High Magick

Angels and Archangels

RITUAL

AN ESSENTIAL GRIMOIRE

DAMIEN ECHOLS ✴ LORRI DAVIS

sounds true
BOULDER, COLORADO

Boulder, CO 80306

© 2022 Damien Echols and Lorri Davis

Sounds True is a trademark of Sounds True, Inc.

This book is not intended as a substitute for the medical recommendations of physicians, mental health professionals, or other health-care providers. Rather, it is intended to offer information to help the reader cooperate with physicians, mental health professionals, and health-care providers in a mutual quest for optimal well-being. We advise readers to carefully review and understand the ideas presented and to seek the advice of a qualified professional before attempting to use them.

Published 2022

Case design by Lisa Kerans
Book design by Linsey Dodaro
Cover sigil, signatures, runes, and talisman illustrations by Damien Echols and Lorri Davis
Practice and Rose Cross illustrations by Meredith March

Printed in Canada

BK06254

Library of Congress Cataloging-in-Publication Data
Names: Echols, Damien, author. | Davis, Lorri, author.
Title: Ritual : an essential grimoire / Damien Echols and Lorri Davis.
Description: An essential grimoire. | Boulder, CO : Sounds True, [2022] | Includes bibliographical references.
Identifiers: LCCN 2021035650 (print) | LCCN 2021035651 (ebook) | ISBN 9781683648208 (hardcover) | ISBN 9781683648215 (ebook)
Subjects: LCSH: Magic. | Ritual. | Grimoires.
Classification: LCC BF1623.R6 E28 2022 (print) | LCC BF1623.R6 (ebook) | DDC 133.4/3--dc23

LC record available at https://lccn.loc.gov/2021035650

LC ebook record available at https://lccn.loc.gov/2021035651

10 9 8 7 6 5 4 3 2 1

TO TAMI SIMON,
WHO BROUGHT US BACK TO LIFE

CONTENTS

INTRODUCTION

GROUNDED
IN RITUAL

The need for ritual is innate. It is born of a deep need to articulate our times of transition, our profound experiences. It is an essential part of what makes and keeps us human. Rituals can act as the punctuation marks in our life, providing us with a sense of structure.

Humans are ritualistic. We use rituals to frame our lives, even when we don't realize that we've built our lives around them. For me, ritual has been an anchor, a buffer from the outside world.

As a child I was fearful. Scared of interactions with others, my first day of school ended abruptly after I threw up at the threshold of my first grade class.

Once I was able to keep the butterflies in my stomach at bay, I realized that there were things I could control all around me. I could sit in the same chair each day. I could eat the same lunch, and I could have my lunch at the same table, day after day. These things I could count on kept me grounded.

The realization that I could calm my nerves by living my life in a ritualistic way got me through many transitions.

I began using ritual to heal after my husband Damien got off death row in 2011. I'd worked on his case, managing a huge legal team and partnering with supporters from around the world in the work that would eventually see him freed.

What we weren't prepared for was the total destruction of our relationship, our health, and our ability to live productive lives after the locusts of complex PTSD took their toll.

Five years later, we had traveled the world promoting books and films and giving public talks. We'd moved five times. Through it all Damien was barely functioning. His traumatic brain injury went unseen by most. He presented as healthy and capable, but inside he was as frightened and savage as a wild animal trapped in a corner. Reeling in fear, I exacerbated his condition by fighting and blaming. Finding ourselves suicidal, we eventually sought therapy, but most importantly, we began to rebuild our lives through ritual. I'm happy to say that not only did we survive, but we are thriving, and I attribute it all to God and the rituals that we have built our lives around.

Many of the rituals you'll find in this book are the very same we used to come back to life. We collected them together in this grimoire to give everyone access to the healing power of magick.

WELCOME

Humans have performed rituals since the dawn of civilization. Those ritual actions created grounding points that enabled divine energy to enter the physical realm. This is exactly what ritual magick offers to us today.

Rituals are moments when we acknowledge this life is a vehicle we are using to break the chains that bind us to fate. They are actions we carry out in order to marry the energies of the heavens to the energy of the earth. In essence, rituals are the way we gradually lift ourselves out of an unsatisfactory, distracted, and purely materialistic way of interacting with life, and instead walk with one foot in each world. It's through ritual that we each become our own priest and sovereign. In magick we use rituals to unite that which is above with that which is below to achieve completion of the Great Work, that is, crystallizing all of the levels and layers of the aura so that they survive the death of the physical body.

Defeating death probably sounds like a lot more than you bargained for when you picked up this book, but even the most basic ritual teaches us that we are never truly

powerless. With repetition, a ritual allows us to exert more and more control over the reality we are creating until even a prison cell can begin to feel like a control tower from which you can reach out, touch the world, and bring about change. Ritual not only allows us to wield divine energy to change the world, but also to create our own world and dwell within it.

When I first started having success with magickal rituals, I still doubted myself and was tempted to chalk it up to coincidence. However, as the years went by and I experienced more and more results, I eventually not only lost any doubts I had but became more surprised if it didn't work than if it did.

In my previous books I have written about magick as the Western path to enlightenment. I am convinced that all of the modern Abrahamic religions—Judaism, Christianity, and Islam—are actually vehicles used to pass along the same coded information. The whole point of the story of Jesus was to make this ancient magickal information more available so that anyone could become a king. He was bringing an end to the "divine right" of kings to rule, giving everyone keys to obtaining sovereignty over their own existence. This is why magick is called the "royal science." It is the means by which a slave can become a monarch.

In magick, when we say, "God created the world," it means something different than when religions use that phrase. In magick, think of the word "God" as shorthand for that infinite consciousness that lies outside the boundaries of time and space. It is eternal, without borders, qualities, or characteristics. In order to experience any sort of change, it must pour itself into the boundaries of material existence.

God didn't just create the world, it became the world. It became us. This is why the Bible says that God gave humans dominion over the earth—because we were meant to continue the process of creation, to pick up where Source left off and continue attempting to create heaven on earth. This is the meaning behind the part of the Lord's Prayer that says, "Thy kingdom come, thy will be done, on earth as it is in heaven."

Trust me, I'm well aware that the Abrahamic traditions may have left a bad taste in the mouths of those who have experienced their more oppressive aspects. They may have left you with no desire to work with any system that reminds you of them. I myself once felt that way. But this system predates all of those religions. In fact, those religions pretty much hijacked the system entirely from the ancient Sumerians and just put a new spin on it—same as when they built cathedrals and churches on top of ancient pagan holy sites. None of that really matters when it comes to the rituals in this book. You won't find a lot of arcane terminology or lengthy ceremonies here. What you will find are simple practices to develop your own connection to the energy and intelligence of the universe, whether you are on the path to becoming a full-fledged mage or are completely new to working with subtle energy.

Wherever you are on your journey, welcome.

PART 1

WORKING
WITH ENERGY

Here's the way magick works: even though infinite consciousness manifests itself in time and space, there is still an endless amount of it that lies outside the material plane. It's all around us and within us, and we are within it, much like fish in the ocean. It has a kind of intelligence embedded within it and behaves as we program it to behave. It shapes itself to conform to our expectations. We can draw upon this infinite energy source that saturates the universe by using our breathing and visualization. In this first section all of the rituals are about developing these basic skills of energy work.

When we're working with subtle energy, we're working with a substance that exists on the etheric, or astral, level of reality. This level of reality overlaps and interpenetrates the physical but is more ephemeral. It's said in magick that anything and everything that exists on the material plane began as energy on the astral plane and eventually became dense enough to gradually come into being in the physical. This is why shaping energy is such a vital aspect of magick to master—because you can use this energy to shape the world around you. This may sound too good to be true, but we're not here to convince you of it or convert you to a way of believing. Instead, Lorri and I will just give you the methods to try it for yourself.

What exactly is this energy we're working with and shaping? Its name has varied from culture to culture throughout time, but it has always been known—as well as the techniques to accumulate it and cultivate it. In fact, it was at the very heart of the ancient Sumerian culture and religion. They called it "*melam*" or "*melammu*" and said it made those who practiced accumulating it glow like a star on the astral plane. It was often said this *melam* was like a "garment" made of light. This garment was also at the heart of Christianity. When Christ revealed this garment (called the "solar body" in magick) to his disciples on the mountaintop during the episode known as the transfiguration, they fell on the ground in terror.

This is why the Sumerians translated the word *melam* to mean "fearsome radiance" as well as "aura." In cuneiform, *melammu* was written with the ideogram for "fire," which ties into the Sumerian metaphors about the gods being clothed in fire and light. To this day, thousands of years later, modern magicians still sometimes refer to this energy as "astral light." The ancient priest-kings of Sumeria practiced rituals to gather as much of this energy around themselves as possible, so that they could disperse it out to the masses. They credit it with all sorts of amazing qualities that we receive when we accumulate large quantities of it, including physical vitality and longevity, charisma, beauty, pleasure, sex appeal, willpower, and independence. *Melammu* also translates into "divine radiance." Those who are perceptive to this astral light, as mages in the 1800s called it, see it as a psychic light shining from the person.

This divine light is what artists of old were attempting to illustrate when painting halos around figures like saints and archangels. Everyone actually has this "light" shining from within them, which we usually call an aura in the West. The difference in those who are in closer contact with divinity is that their aura begins to shine with a much more brilliant intensity. This happens due to ingesting energy on the astral level of reality for spiritual sustenance. When we begin using parts of ourselves that extend beyond the material plane of reality, those parts grow stronger and more a part of our experience of the world as a result.

Working with the internal energy system to induce higher states of consciousness has been known in every age of mankind and is still practiced in some cultures through tai chi, chi gung, and yoga. In the western tradition it's done through magick. Author and teacher Dion Fortune defined magick as "the Yoga of the West."

Dion Fortune was the equivalent of a tai chi master within the magickal tradition. She described a whole and healed aura "as sure a defense against psychic invasion as the healthy and unbroken skin is a defense against bacterial infection." One of the benefits of doing energy work is that it can repair the aura, healing it of rips and wounds. It was this kind of energetic repair that kept me alive during some of my hardest times on death row. In my early days of learning magick, I found that what I loved most was working with energy using visualization and breathwork. I experienced amazing results, which is what made me love it so much. This work is incredibly effective and can be done in ways that are far less static than sitting meditation.

In ancient Chinese Taoist teachings, it was said, "All that is necessary is to circulate the light." The sages of that tradition have said that if you just focus on mastering how to take in and work with the light, then everything else will take care of itself. Let's get to it.

NOURISHING THE AURA

Magick teaches that we never use our own energy to effect change, because doing so would eventually deplete our system. Instead, we use energy taken in from the infinite Source by using breathwork and visualization. This is a simple exercise for helping to nourish our entire energy system with fresh energy and remove energetic blockages.

Take a comfortable position.

Close your eyes and focus your attention
on the center of your chest—right
about where your heart is.

Envision a twelve-inch sphere of gold light
glowing brilliantly in the center of your chest.
It encompasses both your heart and your
solar plexus, a perfect balance of love and
power. This is the primary energy center we
will be working with throughout this book.

Inhale slowly three times, each time
envisioning the gold sphere in your chest
growing brighter and brighter. Each time
you exhale the air goes out—but the chi you
have inhaled stays in the golden sphere.

After the third inhalation, envision the
energy you've been inhaling and holding in
the gold sphere radiating out of the sphere
and spreading out through your body and
aura. Imagine that it feels like very warm,
golden lava as it spreads through you.

Don't worry if you can't "see" the sphere. Start out
by just imagining it as best as you can. Everyone
"visualizes" in their own way. You may feel the
energy more than see it in your mind's eye, for
example. This doesn't mean you're doing it wrong.

Repeat this process three times upon arising
from bed each morning for more energy
and clarity as you go through your day.

THE FOURFOLD
BREATH

Normal breathing consists of two parts: the intake of breath, and the exhalation of breath. The body does this unconsciously, just as the heart beats. While the body breathes with no conscious effort, the breath can also be regulated at will to help ease many emotional responses. Such regulation is an essential skill for practicing magick, which is why I'm including this ritual here even though Damien included several versions of it in *High Magick*.

The Fourfold Breath can be useful in avoiding rage. It can also be useful at the onset of panic attacks, or it can help get one to sleep at night. It's an excellent preparation for meditative practices and is my go-to any time I want to calm and change the chemistry of my mind.

To do the Fourfold Breath, you breathe in for a count of four seconds, then hold for a count of four seconds, then breathe out slowly for four seconds, then hold the breath with no air for a count of four seconds. If you're panicky, your breath may be shallow at first. It's fine to adjust the speed of your counting as needed. Do it for a few cycles and you'll begin to relax into slower breathing.

Here is a special version of the Fourfold Breath to help hone your visualization skills and connect you to the natural cycles of the year.

Find a restful position in which you can relax.

As you breathe in to a count of four, think of spring—flowers, cool showers, the bright green of new leaves, bugs and birds coming alive with noise. Hold for four seconds as you bring to mind the scents, sounds, sights, tastes, and sensations of glorious springtime.

As you breathe out for four seconds, summer arrives—hot sun, cool swimming pools, vibrant colors, warm evenings, ice cream. Hold for four seconds as you immerse yourself in your sense of summer.

Breathe in again for four as autumn
comes—crisp evenings, apple orchards,
brilliantly colored leaves, pumpkins. Hold
for four seconds as you feel into fall.

As you exhale for four, winter arrives—cold, frosty
mornings, snow, hot chocolate, evergreen trees
covered in snow. Hold for a count of four before
letting spring return with your next in-breath.

Repeat this cycle as many times as you wish.

HOW TO
PRAY

I've been praying for a long time. Growing up in a fundamentalist Christian church taught me about prayer, but it always felt as if there was no energy in the stream of words being thrown from the pulpit. They were filled with anger and repentance, and there was nothing about joy or abundance. No wonder I spent most of my time back in my pew inventing machines in my head that would carry the preacher away to another place. He wouldn't be hurt, no, just whisked into a chamber by a special broom-like device and from there be transported to the local Kmart or Long John Silvers. Just far enough away that an uncomfortable silence would descend, then we would all file out and I could go on home to watch Walt Disney.

I stopped praying for an episode in my life when I lost touch with the Divine. What I didn't understand during that time was that God hadn't let go of me. Thinking back over the many times I put myself in danger and walked out unscathed, I see that I was divinely protected. I have been led to people and situations through signs and symbols or various other means; God was working in my life. Through a film I was brought to Damien. Coincidences don't exist, but when one is careening through life, there is the possibility of missing great moments. Prayer to me is essential in creating my life through God.

I heard bestselling author and geologist Gregg Braden give a talk about prayer that changed my life. He explained how a very effective means of prayer is to *feel* what it's like to have a prayer answered. His advice to a community praying for rain in a devastating drought was to experience prayer through all of the senses. First, he said, think of wanting the rain, then actually feel the excitement of storm clouds gathering—see in your mind's eye the dark gray clouds, the lightning flashing. Then feel the wind pick up and the sense of coolness that comes with impending rain, a shift in the atmosphere. Actually imagine the first drops landing on the parched earth, on your skin. Taste the raindrops on your tongue. Finally, feel the downpour, the rain driving hard on the landscape, the relief coming from the trees, the joy at finally having everything become new in the cleansing, nourishing, abundant rain.

The whole time he was talking, I could feel it!

I've done visualizing for a while now. Damien laughed when I told him I had often visualized him sitting beside me on a plane when he was in prison. I did it so many times, which is why he figures we've traveled so often! But to condense a prayer into a feeling, and then to imagine all of the components of what make up the experience of that, through all of our senses—that was new to me, and very exciting.

In every moment of our lives we are feeling. Whatever we feel becomes our prayer, and it signals what we want in our lives. If we're feeling fear, anger, joy, or overwhelming gratitude—these are the things that will be mirrored back to us. Our very lives are in prayer all of the time.

Visualization and prayer therefore work best when you draw on your own lived experiences. You can use your own positive memories to create a ritual for joy or any other desired experience.

For example, I grew up swimming and most of my happiest memories and moments of clarity have come while in water. As a child I would launch off the bottom of the pool, my toes pushing into the slightly rough surface, propelling myself up out of the water while in my head singing a very corny country song about being the happiest girl in the world. The water droplets reflecting the sun in a spray of golden light, the brilliance of bursting into that world of blue and yellow light was exhilarating.

Swimming is like seeing a movie to me. There is something about being immersed in light and movement. Afterward I feel something has shifted. The difference is the way I feel—elated, light, and inspired. Give this a try, or make your own ritual based on a memory:

Imagine yourself in a pool or a body of
water you love to swim in where you can
touch the bottom with your toes.

Visualize swimming down to the bottom
and launching yourself up, up, up through
the water into the sunlight where
your energy bursts forth into joy.

Erupt out of the water with a favorite song
that brings a feeling of joy or inspiration, or
simply let out a YAWP to the universe.

If you practice this over and over, you will feel a sense
of elation and a natural feeling of being energized by the
water, movement, and the bright light of the sun.

TREE OF LIFE ENERGIZING RITUAL

You'll be amazed at the vitality and clean energy this simple visualization and breathing ritual creates.

Sit cross-legged on the ground, or in
a chair with your feet on the floor.

From the source of Divinity at the
top of the universe, inhale and draw a
white light into your heart center.

As you exhale, imagine the light shooting
down your body, and through your feet,
forming roots that go deep into the earth.

Inhale white light from the Source above your
head into your heart center. On this exhale, shoot
that energy up through the top of your head
and imagine branches growing and arching
down to touch the earth, like a weeping willow.

Now imagine the center of the earth as a huge
ball of green light. Inhale and bring that green
light up through your roots and your body. Let it
shoot out the top of your head into your branches,
which take the light back down into the earth.

Repeat this cycle ten times and
then go about your day.

DIRECTING ENERGY TO THE HANDS

When beginning magickal training, the first thing that most people learn to focus on is their hands. Once you are capable of consciously directing energy to the hands, it's only a short step to direct it through the hands and use it for all sorts of other purposes, such as charging items, healing, creating shields to protect and defend your aura, and countless other uses.

Begin by rubbing the palms together briskly
for thirty seconds, or until you feel them
beginning to grow warm. When you do
this, you're waking up and stimulating
major energy centers in the hands.

Next, close your eyes and focus on the golden
sphere-shaped energy center in the middle
of your chest. Take several deep, even breaths
while visualizing that you are pulling chi or
energy from the world around you with every
inhalation. With every breath, the golden
sphere in your chest grows brighter and brighter
as it is filled with this life-giving energy.

After several breaths—at least three, but I
often do it for as many as ten—you want
to begin sending energy down your arms
and to your hands with every exhalation.

When you inhale, see the sphere
in your chest glow brighter.

When you exhale, see gold light spill out of
the energy center, down your arms, and into
your hands. See it begin filling your hands with
gold light, saturating them so that it appears
in your mind's eye as if your hands are so filled
with gold light that they're surrounded by it.

Every time you inhale you pull in more light, and
every time you exhale it travels down to fill your
hands so that they glow even more brightly.

You should practice this several times a day, until you
can see it clearly in your mind. You should also do it a
few times when you're preparing to either send or receive
energy with your hands. You can add tactile sensations to
help with the visualization. For example, as you see the
gold light move down your arms and into your hands,
imagine that it feels like warm water or lava as it moves.
Adding other senses to the visualization will strengthen
its effects.

ENERGY
CIRCULATION
WITH OTHERS

When I was in prison I used to practice energy circulation techniques with those who came to visit me. Sometimes there would be as many as four people and myself in the prison visitation room, eyes closed and focused on our breathing and internal visualizations. Other times it would just be Lorri and me doing it to stay calm and give us something to focus on when we were being harassed by guards.

There are all sorts of reasons to do energy circulation with others. For one thing, it's a sharing of one another's vital essence. In a situation where I was low and depleted of energy, it gave me a boost and kept me going. Another reason is for practice. The more we work with energy, the more adept we become at generating and directing it—so you want to be doing it constantly, in all different environments, alone and with others.

To do it with two people, sit facing one another with your feet flat on the floor.

Each person holds out their hands, right palm facing down toward the earth and left palm facing up.

The other person's downward-facing right palm rests on your upward-facing left palm, and your downward-facing right palm rests upon their upward-facing left palm. You're now face-to-face with one another, touching palms to complete a circuit.

You each close your eyes and let your attention rest in the center of your chest where you visualize a glowing golden orb that looks like the sun at noon, encompassing both your heart and solar plexus.

Every time you inhale, visualize yourself pulling
in chi or energy from the universe around
you and into the golden sphere in your chest.
With each inhalation it grows brighter and
brighter gold, packed with more and more
energy. Do this about six to ten times, just
to get the energy center flushed with chi.

Once you feel ready, you inhale and
see the golden orb in your chest glow
as bright as you can make it. Hold the
breath for a couple of seconds.

Then, as you exhale, see the golden light you have
been inhaling into your chest spill from your
golden orb, down your left arm, out your left
hand, and up your partner's right arm. It comes
to a stop inside the golden sphere in their chest.

Hold your breath on the exhale for a
couple of seconds. As you begin inhaling
again, see the flow of light continue from
the sphere in their chest, down their left
arm, out of their palm, and into yours.

It continues up your right arm and back
into the gold sphere in the center of your
chest. Continue this process through several
rounds—aim to do it for five to ten minutes
and build up to longer sessions from there.

As you exhale, the light exits your chest, goes
down your arm, up your partner's arm, and
into their chest. As you inhale, the light
leaves the energy center in their chest, goes
down their arm, up your arm, and back into
the golden energy center in your chest.

Once you get the hang of it, it's easy to keep up.
You're just inhaling and exhaling, sending energy
back and forth from yourself to your partner.

After you master doing it with one other person, you
can add as many more as you'd like—you just have
everyone sit in a circle touching palms. As you exhale
you send energy to the person on your left. As you inhale you receive it from the person on your right. This
weaves the energy of the group together and can be
powerful to do before having several people put energy into manifesting something together. There are all

sorts of variations that can be done with both energy circulation rituals with others as well as group manifestation projects.

In magick we say that everything in the physical world mirrors everything in the energetic plane. This is the meaning behind "as above, so below; as within, so without." This means that just as our hands are joined to our chests via our arms, so too are our hand chakras connected to our hearts via meridians. This is why it feels so good to hold hands with someone you love— because you have formed a connection that allows energy to flow back and forth between your heart center and theirs. And it's for this very same reason that it feels so disagreeable to have to shake hands with someone you are really uncomfortable with.

When I talk about how useful it is to master this one single technique it's because there are so many different rituals that can be done with it that it's inexhaustible.

ENERGY CIRCULATION WITH TREES

I n ancient cultures trees were synonymous with longevity since they regularly live for hundreds of years. Considered especially potent were evergreen trees because they never lose their leaves. This made them symbolic of immortality, since they don't appear to die in winter months the way other trees seem to do.

By repetitively sharing energy with them, ancient Taoist energy workers attempted to share in the longevity the trees experience. You do this much the same way you send and receive energy with a person.

Find a healthy adult tree that appears
to be full of life and vitality, and place
the palms of both hands upon it.

Close your eyes and turn inward, focusing on the
golden orb of light in the center of the chest.

As you inhale, see it glow even brighter
gold from the energy you are taking
in from the world around you.

Hold your breath for a moment as you see the
golden energy center glow brilliantly. As you
exhale, golden light travels down your arms, out
of your hands, and into the trunk of the tree.

See the light extend down your arms and into
the tree as if it were tentacles connecting your
energy center to the green chi within the tree.
Envision the tree as full of brilliant, green light.
This is the natural energy created by the tree.

As you begin to slowly inhale, pull the brilliant
green light from the tree, up both arms, and
into the energy center in your chest.

As you exhale, the energy moves from your
chest, back down your arms, and returns
to the tree. Do this at least ten times.

Inhale and pull energy from the tree into the
orb in your chest. Exhale and see the energy
flow back down your arms and into the tree.

To end the exercise, inhale one final time, and
pull energy from the tree into the golden, glowing
center in your chest. Hold your breath to the
count of four. As you exhale, see the light in the
center of your chest radiate out and saturate
every cell in your body, as well as fill your entire
aura, with brilliant, rejuvenating golden energy.

ANGELIC
ENERGY

Statistically, more people believe in angels than believe in God. That belief is what puts so much energy into angel magick and makes it so effective. Mankind's belief in angels is as old as its most ancient gods, dating back to the earth's very first cities. But as those gods were forgotten and succumbed to time, the belief in angels flourished and transformed.

An angel is essentially just subtle energy that has taken on the particular definitions that we have imposed upon it. We tend to look at angels as being benevolent protectors who act on behalf of our highest good. We have deeply ingrained programming in our psyche that angels will not do anything that would harm us or others. We tend to believe they will act in our best interest and provide us with protection. And since that's what we expect, for the most part that's what we get. Angels are the very substance from which what we think of as reality is formed, and that substance is both malleable and intelligent.

Those who have come to my classes, talks, and retreats in the past have heard me speak about the very first time I ever perceived an angel, and how unsettling it was. I was still on death row and had decided that I was going to do the Lesser Banishing Ritual of the Pentagram three times a day for thirty days. This is a detailed ritual that calls upon the four major archangels. You're essentially in the center of four giant archangels that protect you from all sides.

It was after doing this for several days when I suddenly began to perceive something I could not quite articulate. When I say that I "saw" something, I don't mean with my physical eyes. Instead, I'm referring to suddenly becoming aware that I was using more than the senses I had grown accustomed to using in the material world. In hindsight, I realize this is another side effect of doing rituals involving energy work—it greatly increases your psychic intuition. By *psychic*, I don't mean the sort of thing you see on a bad TV show. When I use the word *psychic*, what I'm referring to is your ability to perceive and detect subtle energy.

When you begin to be aware of it, it changes the way you interact with the universe around you, because you suddenly know to the deepest level of your being that the material world is not all that there is to reality.

On page 237 you'll find a chart that corresponds each of the four major archangels to their counterparts in the physical world, things like the elements, the directions, and colors. In magick, certain colors, names, scents, herbs, stones, etc., all correspond to various angels. By incorporating those correspondences into our energy work, we incorporate the qualities of the angels associated with them into the work as well.

Novice magicians memorize these correspondences, as they are the ingredients for creating any ritual. Working with angels in this way is like doing calisthenics for our energy system and has all sorts of side effects, like being more relaxed, calm, and peaceful. Your relationships with others and the world as a whole will become more harmonious. And you'll deal with the drama and conflict you come into contact with in a much more skillful way. For now, try this simple ritual any time you need divine assistance.

It doesn't matter if you sit or stand, and you can call on the angels anywhere—on a train, in an elevator, at the office.

Face east, if it's possible to know which direction
it is. If not, imagine you are facing east.

Breathe in and invoke the Archangel Michael
to your right. You "invoke" by imagining
a vibrant red color. You can also say to
yourself "I call on the Archangel Michael."

On your next inhale, invoke the Archangel Uriel
to your left. The color will be bright green.

Next, breathe in and invoke the
Archangel Raphael in front of you. A
brilliant gold light appears.

Lastly, breathe in and invoke the Archangel
Gabriel behind you. A flood of blue appears.

Invoking the Archangels in this way and knowing you
are surrounded by their wisdom and protection is a wonderful, quick way to engage with them at any time of day,
in any circumstance.

USING
ELEMENTAL
ENERGIES

I n a 2002 experiment reported by the Harvard
Gazette, conducted in Normandy, France, two
monks from the Buddhist tradition wore sen-
sors that recorded changes in heat production and
metabolism.

The thinly clad monks sat in forty-degree tempera-
tures and had wet, freezing cold sheets draped over
them. Using a yoga technique known as Tummo, they
entered a state of deep meditation. It wasn't long before steam began rising from the sheets. As a result of
body heat produced by the monks during meditation,
the sheets dried in about an hour.

The monks believe that the energy generates warmth as it accumulates and becomes an inner fire or inner heat that burns away the dross of ignorance and ego-clinging.

The purpose of Tummo is to gain control over body processes during practice of the "highest yoga tantra," which leads to enlightenment. Tummo is the fierce goddess of heat and passion in the Tibetan Buddhist tradition and is a Tibetan word for inner fire.

Monks who practice Tummo describe visualizations of "blazing and dripping."

I would never want to disrespect what these monks are doing in their holy practice. But I was intrigued about how this relates to magickal rituals that draw on the energy of the elements.

I began to ponder how a fire visualization could be used in conjunction with everyday activities and ordinary goals—like my desire to fit into a certain little black dress in my closet. Then I seized upon an idea that has become one of my regular rituals.

Before I exercise, I imagine a match lights the flame of an inner brazier that runs under my skin. It's a pleasurable feeling as I imagine it spreading throughout my arms, legs, belly—all the areas where I tend to carry extra weight.

As I run stairs or walk, the tiny flames melt
away unwanted fat. As I build up heat, I
envision it all being expelled when I exhale.
The faster the breath comes, the more I burn
off. You can add a visualization to this. "See"
the fat burning off and being expelled through
your breath as a yellowish substance.

Always remember to turn the brazier off
when you are finished exercising.

I enjoy doing the "brazier" visualization, and I've
noticed a huge difference in my workouts and the outcome. I feel certain I'm working less hard for more
satisfying results.

Many traditions, Tibetan Buddhism and magick included, speak of how we are made up of the elements, as
is the entire universe. Each element has its own particular qualities and correspondences. We can draw on the
elements for support and incorporate their energies into
our rituals. You'll find a chart of elemental correspondences on page 234.

I believe there is no limit to what we can do with energy work and visualization. If I can feel a bit better in my
little black dress, well, all the better.

DRAWING ON THE ENERGY OF PLACES

There are locations where you can find condensed pockets of energy that can be absorbed, used, or just appreciated. One of those places in NYC is known as the Cloisters. It's a series of medieval monasteries that were brought over from Europe by John D. Rockefeller Jr. and reassembled near the northern end of Manhattan into one large sacred artifact. Housed within it you can find reliquary busts that house the skulls of female saints, the stone sarcophagus of a knight from the crusades, and a courtyard that was designed to be so beautiful that it reminds pilgrims of the Garden of Eden. Visitor's thoughts are turned to angels from the moment they enter, and their eyes meet the painting of an androgynous Archangel Michael driving a spear through the face of a demon. People have looked upon this piece for over five hundred years and mulled over the existence of these celestial intelligences. That kind of faith carries an incredibly strong energetic charge. Millions of eyes, minds, and hearts have put so much energy into this piece that it has become one of the most powerful archangel talismans on earth. Being in proximity to artifacts like that can have incredibly beneficial results to our consciousness.

I began regularly visiting the Cloisters after someone once said to me—"If you want to have fine, beautiful, meaningful things in your life, then you have to surround yourself with things and places that have that energy." So I'd go there regularly to just linger and allow myself to be bathed and saturated by the energy of the place. The centuries of energy that built up there can be absorbed to strengthen the aura. You can do it actively, by using breathwork and visualization, or you can do it passively just by spending time there—because we are constantly, automatically absorbing the energy of the places and people we are near. I think places or things that have accumulated a lot of energy around them (of either the good or bad sort) tend to psychically draw people to them. This is why over seven million people a year are drawn to visit the Met. It's basically a storage facility for a big chunk of the world's most powerfully charged talismans and magickal artifacts. When you walk those halls, you are literally walking among gods. Deities of every nation, people, and period of time are now all coexisting under one roof.

Here is a simple practice for drawing in the energy of a room or a place:

Get still and concentrate on your breathing.

As you take in breath, "see" it form a sphere of white light in the center of your chest, or your heart center.

Now, take in another deep breath and take the energy of the room into your heart center. Let it take on the color you imagine the place feels like; for example, a church may "feel" purple, and a classroom may "feel" yellow.

As with other rituals, imagine that this energy flows through you and into the center of the earth, where it will remain for you to draw on as needed.

PART 2

GROUNDING & PURIFICATION

Often when people are new to energy work they forget or neglect to do regular grounding techniques. I've even heard people say they deliberately don't practice any grounding technique because they don't want to be "tied to this world."

That's not what grounding actually does, although I can see why the name would perhaps make one think of it that way. When we practice regular grounding, we actually increase the health and vibrancy of the aura by eliminating harmful or lower vibrational energy. We allow those energies to be consumed by the earth and transmuted into something else. The earth is a natural recycler of energy, constantly turning the old and dead growth into nutrients to feed new cycles. She'll happily take in whatever energy we wish to discard and will change it into something that will nourish and heal. Grounding is therefore closely related to and essential for the purification of the body, mind, and spirit.

Everything on the energy level mirrors everything on the physical level. For example, every time you inhale, you then exhale. If you drink water, you then must urinate. If you only take in, the consequences will be dire. The same can be true of holding in harmful energy. We take in energy from many sources—from people, from places—and that energy isn't always beneficial. It may leave a residue that will build up over time, causing illness, physical pain, or disconnection from joy and love. It's this build-up of negative energetic residue that needs to be released into the earth to be recycled. Grounding rituals are crucial to keeping our energy bodies clean and healthy, which is in turn essential for effectively practicing magick.

These practices work best in the moment. Right when you feel angry or stressed, ground it out. This takes practice and discipline, because once anger takes over, it short-circuits logic and reason. Through repetition, we can learn to ground out these harmful energies when they arise, thus eliminating the more unsavory outcome of marinating in them. Lingering or obsessing on emotions such as anger or shame creates even more harm. Learning to ground in the moment leads to living in the moment, thereby mastering your emotions.

Another reason to ground is to thwart the ego, which loves stress because it strengthens the illusion of duality; there's you and the person with whom you're angry, there's you and the thing you fear. Duality strengthens the ego's boundaries. Ultimately, there's only a singularity, one consciousness manifesting in trillions of different points, but we don't experience reality in that way most of the time because the boundaries created by the ego are so dense. So even though grounding looks like basic energetic hygiene, like brushing your teeth or taking a shower, it's incredibly useful for transcending duality and eventually experiencing your true self.

You can exert control over the energy fields surrounding you with your will alone. Your energy naturally tends to follow the patterns laid out by your mind, so when you think of your aura doing something, it will automatically begin trying to do that very thing. The more we practice, the more powerful that effect becomes. As you learn the following rituals for grounding, you'll note that some are different ways for doing what seems to be the same thing. Try each one to distinguish which ones

work best for you, then choose one or more to practice
regularly and apply in moments of need.

LITERAL GROUNDING

Many times while Damien was on death row I would spin out. Not having any control over a situation that was life-threatening to a loved one played havoc with my emotions.

My stress levels affected Damien's stress levels, and over time we became rather frayed at the edges.

At that time, I was living in a house situated in the woods. Damien suggested I go out and sit on the ground when things began to twist and turn in my psyche.

I can still visualize it, and I go there in my mind even to this day. The forest was tall pines with some oak strewn about. The ground was hard but covered in pine needles. I sat with my back against the shaggy bark of a well-established evergreen.

I sat. I breathed. I closed my eyes and cleared my mind. And slowly I began to feel calm.

To ground yourself on the actual earth, with its soil and leaves, and in deep, deep silence is like no other medicine.

You can do it in your mind while in a cab or waiting in the doctor's office. It doesn't have to be pines and oak; it can be sand with the sound of waves crashing. The important thing is to connect with the earth.

Find your place on the ground and breathe.

SINK
INTO EARTH

Here is a very simple and powerful ritual for
grounding with the earth while indoors.

Lie on the floor and relax.

Visualize that your body is sinking into the
ground, down, down through all the layers
of soil, through the bedrock, down, down
to the center of the earth, to the lava that
will burn out all of your impurities.

After your "cleaning," pull your body back up
through the earth to the floor. Arise renewed.

GROUNDING
WITH WATER

I t's not hard to incorporate grounding practices into
your everyday routine.

When taking a shower, as the water falls
over you, envision it as white light raining
down. It not only flows over your body, it
flows through your body, like a rain shower
of light, cleaning out your energy body.

Imagine the water pushing the black accumulated
gunk down, down to the drain, where it continues
to the center of the earth. There it turns a brilliant
green, becoming beneficial to the whole planet.

It brings a whole new meaning to
feeling clean after a shower!

You can also apply this technique in the
bath. As you rest in a hot tub, try to feel that
the water around you is pulling out all of
the impurities from your body in the form
of a dark gray residue. There's a suction-like
energy removing fear, illness, judgment—
everything that separates us from the Divine.

After you're finished, stay in the bathtub
as the water drains away. Imagine it
pulling all of the dark matter down the
drain, where it will flow into the center of
the earth to be cleaned and recycled.

VACUUM FOR ANXIETY & OVERWHELM

hrough my experiences of trial and error I realized that I could dissipate a great deal of emotional energy, provided that even in the grip of the emotion I could remember to ground.

It provides invaluable help to me with things like anger, fear, and even physical symptoms like nausea and headache. I simply do the grounding technique while envisioning that particular sensation being vacuumed from my body and transformed by the earth. If I am angry because someone is being rude, I let the anger be my signal to do the vacuum.

You can envision anger flooding through your aura like red ink dropped into clear water—and then visualize the ink being vacuumed from the water down into the earth through the channel that extends from your aura and into the center of the earth. You will notice an immediate decrease in the anger you feel, as well as in the side effects it produces on you physically, such as muscular tenseness. You can do the same thing with fear or anxiety.

The next time you're in a situation that is producing anxiety, extend the cord of light from the bottom of your aura to the center of the earth and see the anxiety being vacuumed out and turned into green light by the earth's core. I usually see it as gray ash being vacuumed out.

The hardest part of this exercise is remembering to do it in the midst of a normally overwhelming emotion. The key to that is practice, practice, and more practice. And don't beat yourself up if you can't remember it at first. However, if you find your mind revisiting an emotional event, that means its energetic residue is still in your aura, and you should still do the exercise to release it.

This is my favorite grounding technique. I've found it to be the most effective by far, and I use it often.

Imagine your aura as an egg-shaped field surrounding your body about arm's length away from you in all directions. This is about how far the average healthy person's detectable aura extends from their body. If you regularly engage in energy practices, it can extend far beyond that. And if you are ill, it can be much smaller than that.

Imagine the bottom of your aura opening and beginning to extend like a tube down into the very center of the earth. At the center of the earth it connects to a giant, vibrant, emerald green sphere of energy. This represents the chi of the earth itself.

The moment the tube extending from your aura attaches to the green sphere in the earth, you feel a vacuum being exerted that pulls all unwanted energy from your entire auric field. It sucks the energy down into the green sphere, which just grows brighter and brighter as it absorbs the unwanted chi.

You can see the unwanted energy as gray smoke
and soot being sucked out of your aura.

Be sure to keep going until all the gray smoke has
been vacuumed from the aura and into the earth.
Don't leave any behind. Envision and try to feel
your aura close back around you on an inhale.

Once you've finished, think to yourself,
I'm now going to open my eyes and go about my day,
but this shaft of light will continue to connect me
to the earth and ground out any harmful energies.

WET~VAC

Damien taught me the Vacuum while he was still in prison. It has become one of the most important rituals for me, one I do every morning. As with any practice, it changed and grew as I realized how powerful the results were.

Keep in mind that the purpose of this practice is to purify your energy body. I find the exercise most effective when I stand, but it can be done anywhere and in any position. I've done it on a subway platform, on a plane, with a group of people, and alone in my bedroom.

Imagine the center of the earth is a powerful vacuum. From it comes a hose, similar to the hose on a wet-dry vacuum cleaner, but this hose attaches to the bottom of your feet.

The second it attaches, you feel a
strong pull on your energy body.

This is where you can begin to call out specific
conditions or behaviors you want eradicated or
dissolved. Ask that hate, bitterness, judgment,
fear, illness, resentment, resistance—anything
that is preventing you from living your divine
purpose, anything that doesn't bring joy
or love—be sucked out by the vacuum.

As the hose attaches, you can see in your mind's
eye dark matter being powerfully pulled out of
you, traveling down a transparent hose to be
consumed by the center of the earth, where it's
recycled into green energy that sustains life.

The power vacuum cleans out every area of your
body. Areas like the mind and the heart can be
especially stubborn, with big, dark gobs of gunk,
but they eventually give way. Any blockages break
up and are whisked away through the hose.

Once the head is completely clean, the energy
of the aura is then sucked down through
the top of the head, and down through the
center of your body, which is also now clean.

When you feel the vacuum has cleaned
everything, the hose detaches and is
pulled back into the center of the earth.
The opening at your feet closes up.

Now draw down gold light from the Source
of all above your head. Breathe in this golden
light three to ten times, filling up your new,
clean body with divine, healing radiance.

The glorious feeling that follows is hard to believe at
first. If you suffer from a toothache, it's suddenly gone.
If you're working on ridding yourself from a particular
strain of fear, you'll find it's fading by the day. If you're
anxious, a quiet calm descends.

Damien used this practice while in prison to help him
with pain when he couldn't see a doctor or obtain med-
ication. I believe it's one of the main reasons his health
wasn't more devastated than it was by his imprisonment.

ROOM
CLEARING

As you might surmise, the Vacuum can help in many ways. Not only can it clean out your energy field, it can clean rooms, modes of travel—the ways are endless. In the previous rituals we've been working with our own energy body in order to release harmful or unwanted energy from our auras. In this exercise, we're going to press on to the next level, changing external energy, such as the energy in a room or an item.

We leave small, and sometimes not-so-small, traces of our energy everywhere we go. Since that energy has been cycled through our system, it contains traces of our thoughts and emotions. This energy drifts off of us much like dead skin cells do as we move from room to room through a house, and the same is true of everyone else's energy.

For example, let's say you enter a room where a disagreement has just occurred. The unmistakable energy of anger lingers. You can very quickly envision a tube connecting the room to the center of the earth, pulling all of the bad energy out of the room and releasing it into the earth where it is recycled into pure, green, beneficial energy. As you withdraw the tube, close up the place where it was connected, and visualize a huge gold light high above. From that Source, gold light is brought into the room. Now it's safe to enter!

Here are more detailed instructions for clearing a room with the Vacuum:

Begin by closing your eyes and envisioning the room enclosed in a sphere of white light. This represents the energetic counterpart of the room's physical presence. Picture it in your mind for a moment, and then begin visualizing it opening at the bottom and forming a cord or channel that extends down deep into the earth's core. At the center of the earth, this cord connects to the giant green sphere of energy that represents the chi of the earth. This is what we sometimes refer to as "Mother Nature."

You are now envisioning the room in a bubble of light, with a cord that connects to a giant green sphere of light at the center of the earth. Once you get really proficient at this you may even feel a kind of "pop," as if the pressure in the room has changed. It is an incredibly subtle sensation that you may not detect at first, but practice will make it more apparent.

Begin visualizing the same sort of energetic vacuum that you performed on your own aura. Try to "feel" the earth exerting a gentle suction that pulls all the polluted or unwanted energy out of the room. Visualize it as gray or black smoke that fills the room and is gradually sucked down through the energetic cord and into the clean, vibrant energy of the earth where it is recycled. Make certain you get ALL of it. See it pulled from every corner, crack, and crevice, down into the earth.

Once the room is clear in your mind's eye, you can either envision the cord being drawn back up and the room's aura closing as you did your own, or you can leave it connected so that it continues to work—so that any unwanted or harmful energy that comes into the room will continue to be drained away. If you want this to happen continually, so that negative energy doesn't build back up, you'll have to reinforce the visualization for at least a few minutes every day.

It also helps if you lay your hands on a wall of the room while doing this practice. Having physical contact with something or someone reinforces any magick being done on it, because we are utilizing every level of reality by incorporating the material plane into the practice.

CLEARING YOUR COMMUTE

I n New York, the subway is dirty, loud, and often filled with human despair. Sometimes the odors are palpable. You can discreetly perform this ritual on the train or any form of public transportation for a safer, more pleasurable commute—even if you can't magickally do away with unpleasant scents.

Imagine drawing a tube up from the center
of the earth to connect to the train. It draws
all of the noxious energy out of the train
car, filling up the center of the earth
with whatever energy it encounters and
turning it green with abundance.

Visualize the Source of all, a huge sphere
of gold light above your head, and bring
gold light from that Source into the train,
filling it up with brilliant gold light.

Notice how suddenly there is a
lightness to your travels.

BLACK STONE
ENERGY
CLEANSE

Certain stones and crystals have an amazing
ability to hold energy. Black tourmaline, ob-
sidian, and quartz crystal are good examples.
With the assistance of the cleansing power of water or
sunlight, such stones can be powerful aids to purification rituals. Try this as an alternative to the methods
based on the vacuuming technique.

Hold the stone in your hands in front of your
chest. Imagine a white light at the top of the
universe. As you inhale, bring that light into
your heart center, and as you exhale, send that
light, along with all the impurities in your energy
body, down your arms and into the stone.

To purify the stone, hold it under the
faucet, letting the water run "through" it
and down the drain to be purified.

Another way to clear the stone is to leave
it in bright sunlight for a few hours.

Note: See pages 236–239 for gemstone correspondences.

BLACK BALL ENERGY CLEANSE

You can do this ritual whether or not you have any crystals to work with.

Imagine a huge source of light above you that represents God. Inhale the white light from that Source into your heart chakra several times, each time seeing it grow brighter.

Now, as you exhale, see that bright light that
has accumulated in your heart center rush down
your arms, taking all of the dark residue with it,
cleaning your energy body and directing it into a
black ball of negative energy between your hands.

You can now drop the ball into the earth,
visualizing it sinking down, becoming
cleansed as it reaches the center of the earth
where it can become beneficial energy.

Another version is to take the ball of light and
toss it up into that Divine Source above your
head, where it will be burned up and recycled.

FIRE BURNING
THROUGH FEET

This is a ritual for purification from the Hermetic
Order of the Golden Dawn, the group respon-
sible for codifying and preserving much of what
is practiced as magick today. This is a simplified version.

Sit on a chair with your hands on your legs and
your feet planted flat on the floor. Imagine a
black sphere of energy encircling your feet. It
should be about twelve inches in diameter.

As you inhale, imagine fire coming up from the
center of the earth, burning your feet and
the black ball around them. Continue to inhale,
bringing a stronger and stronger blaze. When
you exhale, let it feed the flame, making it burn
hotter. The black ball represents your physical
existence. The flames burn as they begin to purify
it. Each breath brings a lighter shade, from
black to gray, lighter and lighter until the ball
becomes a bright, white, crystalline sphere.

Once the light has been purified, open your
eyes, and stamp your foot or clap to ground the
energy and to signify the end of the ritual.

CORD CUTTING

The relationships we have with people, places, and even events all create energetic connections for us. There are toxic relationships, loving connections, and often inspirational ties involved in all our interactions, but sometimes we form energetic connections with things or people that don't serve us.

If we have frequent thoughts about a person or situation, we can be assured an energetic cord has formed that attaches us to that very thing. It works the other way, too. People can send out their tentacles to attach to you and they can draw from you in ways you may not even conceive of, but that can possibly be a drain on your vitality.

This is why I love to start each day with a fresh pruning of cords, assisted by the Archangel Michael.

I sit quietly and clear my mind.

When I've reached that place of peace, away from
stress and thought, I invoke the mighty Michael,
with his red robes and powerful golden sword.

I then ask him to slice through
any cords attached to me.

I feel the force with which he wields the blade.

I imagine the air moves as he cuts through
any connections made by myself or others.

I ask him to tend to my front, back, sides, under
my feet, and above my head—just to make certain
of any sneaky remnant trying to cleave to me.

Afterward I always feel a change, a shift in energy. It feels clean, good, and a perfect way to start the day.

Of course, after you do this, you'll start forming connections all over again; especially with those you love and with whom you spend time. Those connections are quite lovely, but within them can lurk all of the fears and stresses or even illness that we all carry around with us. It's best to clear those away along with the other, more toxic cords.

Cord cutting is also a good reminder to practice magick; to keep your house clean, if you will. That way, when you do connect to others, you can try to keep them and yourself filled with divine light.

PART 3

CENTERING
& BALANCE

Our washer broke during the pandemic. It was at a time when we couldn't safely venture out for anything: food, pharmacy, and decidedly not a laundromat.

I am the daughter of a mechanic who fixed everything around our house. I grew up watching my dad tackle the hardest of mechanical injustices; nary a professional darkened our door.

So I took to video tutorials, hoping I could diagnose the problem. I drained the water and checked the coin catch, a small cup that catches loose trinkets. Ours contained a bobby pin.

I reset the machine's display and talked to my sister, who proclaimed, "Things spring back to life if you unplug them for a while." My thing didn't. I finally came to the heart-deflating awareness that our washer's fate was beyond my control.

I felt despair creeping around the fringes of my mind.

But then I remembered something: Reach for that better-feeling thought.

I had been practicing a new mental regimen for a few weeks. The premise was that if you make joy your purpose, your goal, then everything else you desire in this life will follow.

Joy is easy, even in confinement, when you have someone you love dearly with whom you share a love of each other and God, friends who care for you and send provisions and toys for your cats, groceries delivered, and a roof where you can soak up sun and breathe clean air.

Joy is more of a challenge when things go wrong; this was the perfect opportunity to test my theory that if you take tiny steps toward happiness, the situation will right itself.

So, I ate a chocolate brownie. It was delicious, and while I don't condone eating your feelings, it did give me a tiny lift. I then burrowed into bed with D and took a dreamy nap. Later, Damien called me up to the roof, where the twilight had just begun, and we watched the stars slowly take shape in a dark blue sky, like a celestial Polaroid.

After we came back inside, I texted our neighbor to ask if we could do laundry at her place, and she said yes.

We find our way back to joy, every time.

Our minds want to be somewhere else most of the time. Most people are in the past, in the future, thinking of someone they love or hate, obsessing on something they want or pondering a place they'd rather be. Where attention goes, energy flows.

Performing centering rituals allows us to withdraw our energy from all of these other distractions and pull it into the here and now.

In order to be your true self, to feel the essence of the Now, which is pure consciousness, being in the moment is the only way. To allow our minds to constantly dwell in the past or future disperses our energy and leaves us scattered and unfocused.

The centering rituals I share here are the ones I use to bring my attention back into the Now.

MEDITATION
FOR DEEP
STILLNESS

Rest quietly in a comfortable position. Take a
few deep breaths, and then start the Fourfold
Breath, counting to four with each inhalation,
then four as you hold it, then four as you
exhale, and four as you hold again. Do this
several times until you find yourself relaxed.

Now, close your eyes and imagine in your
mind fireworks. See the bursts of light and
energy, imagine the loud BOOMS that come
with the explosions of light and color.

This dramatic show symbolizes your mind and
the constant stimulus that is going on in there. It
will help to see it in full display before you pull
the plug, so enjoy it for a few more moments.

Now, let the entirety of your mind and body
go dark. All the fireworks are finished, the
crowds have gone home, and the sky is
black, as if there was never even a spark.

Move your attention from your brain
to your chest and let it rest there. It's
dark, black, with no lights at all.

After a few moments, begin to feel your energy. It's
no longer in your head, but you are aware of a still,
very vital energy in your body. Sometimes it helps
to concentrate on your breathing to keep your
attention on the "real" you that dwells in your body.

Take some time and really sink into
yourself. Feel the essence that is you, not
your thoughts, not what you see out your
eyes, but a deep, quiet emergence of self.

Now, feel how that energy that is you is actually
joined to a bigger energy that is everything.
You can't actually feel where your energy
"ends"—it doesn't stop at your skin, does it?
It's as if you are floating in a vast universe
of energy with no end and no beginning.

When you're ready, bring your attention
back to your Fourfold Breath. See the black
expanse in your chest slowly start to light up,
as though dawn is coming. Let the darkness
lift and you're suddenly in white light.

Open your eyes and slowly come back to the Now.

UPON
WAKING

Waking up is the best time to set the tone for the rest of the day. Often, especially if we're experiencing trying times, our first glimpse of consciousness can be met with a feeling of doom or dread. The mind scrambles around, trying to find where we are, how we feel, what day it is, and what experience we are awakening into (sometimes literally, if travel is involved). Here is a waking ritual you can recite, in your mind or aloud, to help you start your day centered in love.

As I become conscious

Before I even set a foot on the floor

Archangel Raphael, fill my heart with joy and love

As I breathe in, my chest fills with golden light

As I breathe out, the light surrounds me

When you practice this ritual before rising, you'll be amazed how quickly a calmness settles into your being.

A RITUAL
BEDTIME

I went through a period of severe insomnia after I left Arkansas. The inability to sleep became a waking nightmare. I tried everything the experts recommend: dark, cool room; warm bath; a screenless bedroom—an endless list of conditions.

I have a theory about insomnia—I believe it's the ego's way of keeping us from finding our way to God, but that's another book.

In desperation, I resorted to Ambien, which took a devastating toll on my mental alertness and memory, and left me feeling hungover for hours, bleeding into days.

I finally came upon the fix I desperately needed: a ritualized bedtime.

My life has become ritualized in an effort to stay in the moment and to build energy around certain aspects of the day that I know will strengthen and purify the energy in and around me.

Starting out the morning with spiritual practices that invoke Divinity sets me up for a positive, prosperous day, but the rituals performed before sleep are of great importance too; perhaps more so. The state of our minds before sleep sets the stage for so many different outcomes. Going to bed stressed or worried results in tossing and turning and a mind that becomes like a rat in a cage.

There are a few moving parts here, so take what you need and leave the rest, or do the entire ritual; either way you will find falling into sleep will be a most pleasant and relaxing experience.

I try to go to bed at the same time every
night. Our bodies love habit and our circadian
rhythms depend on it. Many of us have lost
or destroyed our circadian rhythms with
our work, travel, and nighttime habits.

I do a few yoga positions for sleep right
before I head to the bedroom. You can find
a whole mess of these with a simple internet
search. Any light, gentle stretching will do.

Once in bed, I apply a series of essential oils and hydrosols. These are open to your preference, but I apply lavender to my temples, ylang ylang behind my ears and on my wrists, and cedar on my legs. I finish off with a spray of roman chamomile hydrosol to my face.

If I need to look at a screen, I have special, yellow-tinted glasses to block out the blue light.

With the covers pulled up and the lights out, I start a long, slow Fourfold Breath.

On the rare occasions I'm still not relaxed, I visualize a location—a beach or a city—and I imagine walking, taking in the smallest details, making it real. This allows my mind to disengage, and I fall asleep.

My sleep had been a battleground for many years. I can now say I look forward to the time of going to bed. It's the most peaceful time of the day, and my waking hours are being fed by the magick I do at night. Sometimes it's the seemingly small rituals that create the biggest shifts in consciousness.

FOURFOLD
BREATH FOR
SLEEP

Once you're in bed, begin the Fourfold Breath.
Breathe in for a count of four, hold for a count
of four, breathe out for a count of four, hold for a
count of four. This signals to your body that you're
winding down. You can use any visualization you
like with the breath, or just focus on the breathing
pattern and the sensation of your breathing.

Once your mind is calm, shift to thinking of
things for which you're grateful. These images
will create joy and happiness, which will allow
your mind and body to drift off happily to sleep.

You may also find it helpful to write the reasons for which you're grateful in a journal before bed. The book can be kept next to your bed. Its close proximity and the thoughts you have toward it will build up energy and help you keep the feeling of gratitude, even when you're not writing in it. It's a powerful way to pull your mind back to being grateful.

SLEEPING WITH
THE ANGELS
OF THE MOON

This is an alternative visualization for either falling asleep or if awakened in the night. You can invoke the Angels of the Moon instanta-neously or with the Fourfold Breath:

Invoke the Angels of the Moon by breathing
in and envisioning their presence. They
will be dressed in purple robes. Have them
surround you on all sides, above and below.

Breathe in for four counts as you
invoke a beautiful Angel arrayed in a
deep purple robe on your right.

Breathe out for four counts and take
another four-count breath, invoking
another Angel of the Moon on your left.

Repeat the Fourfold Breath for invoking
Angels in front, back, above, and below you.

Shortly after visualizing these magnificent entities
around you, the velvety darkness of sleep will overtake
you like a slow-moving wave.

TAKE A TRIP TO DREAMLAND

I f the Fourfold Breath does not lull you to sleep, you can try this self-hypnosis technique.

After you're in a comfortable place, beginning to relax, close your eyes and imagine yourself in an agreeable setting.

Now, start to talk to yourself internally, sort of like a voice-over for a film you're creating in your mind. The key is to use the phrase: "And now." Speak just as a hypnotist might speak.

"And now I'm on a beach ..."

"And now I'm wading in the surf ..."

"And now I hear a seagull overhead ..."

Your voice-over should be very slow,
monotone, the way you would sound
if you were drifting off to sleep.

I still use this technique now, even as my sleep has gotten better. It's just a fun way to relax, and I can envision
places and events I want to manifest in my life. Thoughts
turn into beliefs and beliefs become reality if enough energy is being put into them.

Coming to bed one night, I didn't realize Damien was
half asleep, and I thought I woke him up. I apologized,
but he just smiled and said, "That's okay, I wasn't asleep,
I was walking through Soho, looking at all the places I
love and miss."

I laughed, not knowing that as we lay in bed at night, we were having our own private journeys, traipsing about in our minds.

It turns out to be a wonderful way to fall asleep, but it also enhances your ability to visualize. The more detail you put into your imagined environment, the better. For example, notice the cobblestones you're walking on, the color of a door, or what's in a shop window. As you walk, feel the coolness of a breeze, or the warmth of the sun. Notice the smell of fresh bread as you walk past a bakery. The more you involve your senses, the better. Feel every sensation as if you are actually there, in this place, whether it be the beach, a mountain, or your grandmother's garden.

In one of my favorite books, *Hopscotch* by Julio Cortazar, two characters are trying to navigate a meeting in their dreams—to actually dream the same dream together.

Damien doesn't know it, but I plan on surprising him on one of his etheric explorations of Prague.

PREVENTING NIGHTMARES WITH RUSKU

Damien suffered from nightmares for years. Many a night I would be awakened by his cries as he was being chased in his sleep by unimaginable monsters. Considering his past, it's no wonder these horrors would lurk in his subconscious.

To prevent nightmares, he started invoking the Sumerian god, Rusku, who provides protection during sleep. He is symbolized by a glowing lamp, similar to the lamp from which a genie appears.

Since Rusku has come, the nightmares have gone.

To invoke Rusku:

Get comfortable and still in bed.

Breathe in and envision a glowing
lamp sitting beside you.

Imagine it as a beautiful, intricately
designed "Aladdin's lamp." The more
detailed you make the image, the better.

Know that the lamp (Rusku) will be sitting
beside you all night, protecting you from
nightmares or any other nocturnal disturbance.

ESSENTIAL OIL
RITUAL FOR
ANXIETY & FEAR

Spiritual alchemy is concerned with freeing the spiritual self that is trapped within you by the unrefined parts of yourself—your fears, personal beliefs, self-loathing, etc. I've had the most amazing breakthroughs in spiritual development by using my emotions to induce a change in my circumstances.

I first learned about one system for this process from a Reiki master in Little Rock, Arkansas. I was suffering from debilitating fear at the time, mostly linked to Damien's safety, raising money to pay lawyers, and even losing my job. It seemed my every waking moment was overtaken by anxiety, and my emotional distress had become too severe to endure.

The Reiki master taught me how to use essential oils to trigger an alchemical process that, after a few weeks of intense work, brought about enormous relief. You can use any essential oil you wish for this ritual.

Apply a few drops of essential oil to your temples as you think about being anxious or fearful. Really experience these feelings fully while breathing in the scent of the oil.

After a few moments, apply the same oil to your temples again, and summon the feelings of extreme happiness.

That's it.

When I decide to do something, I go all in, so I did this every hour during the day, and a couple of times during the night. It took a few weeks, but my life was transformed and the relief was enormous.

There is something magickal that happens when you do this; it's alchemical, meaning that the lead of your anxiety turns to gold, or peace. Over time it causes an association with happiness when you apply the oil to your temples, and eventually the feelings of fear subside altogether.

You can use this ritual to address many of the things that throw us out of balance and off center. If you're doing work on bolstering your finances, try thinking about the feelings of lack, the fear of not having enough money that plagues you. When you apply the oil a second time, imagine just how exuberant you'll feel when you have more than enough; imagine what you'll do with your new wealth, how you'll celebrate it, how you'll experience the relief of money flowing to you and through you. It also works for anger, or a broken heart. It has to be expected that sometimes the process can take a long time—but it always works. It's all about reaching for a better frame of mind over and over.

CANDLE MAGICK
FOR GRIEF

A friend of mine lost her beloved dog. Anyone who has had the privilege of falling in love with an animal will understand the overwhelming sadness that can come with the loss of their friend.

My friend's dog, Pete, was a scruffy, dark gray curmudgeon who caused her all kinds of grief from his mischief, but he was one of the loves of her life. I knew when the time came for him to pass it was going to be hard.

This friend works with a company that makes handblown glass votive candleholders. Each of these pieces of art comes with a message, and the colors are heavenly.

After Pete died, she placed one of her beautiful votive candles on her windowsill each evening and lit a candle to remember him. She told me it helped her deal with her grief, it enabled her to feel connected to him, even if his physical body was no longer with her.

You can do this for any situation; for grief, for missing a loved one who's far away, for belief in a dream. Simply choose a candle that feels right, find a quiet place where you can contemplate and make a ritual out of the moments you sit with the candle, meditating on whomever or whatever you're focused on.

MOMENTS LIVED IN LIGHT

How did something so obvious, so rational, manage to elude my consciousness for so long? That change takes time.

Changing the way you think takes time. Believe me, I've been working on it for years; and while I see results, it really did astonish me to realize that my thinking had come from years and years of hardwired, unrestrained resentment, anger, jealousy, rage . . . and that it takes time to transform.

If you were to go back to your childhood home and see the way the people lived, look at what was around you then, what you did, with whom you surrounded yourself, and then think of where you are now—what would you observe?

Life is in continuous movement. Where you are today is so far from where you were as a child, and if you continue to be mindful of reaching your "destiny" (which in itself is in constant change) your experiences will continue to unfold into an endless stream of new manifestation.

The tricky part about looking back is to stay conscious of the Now, to stay in the present as you look back.

> *But Lot's wife looked back,*
> *and she became a pillar of salt.*
> Genesis 19:26

The Bible is full of directives for *thinking*. She looked back, and her life came to a standstill. No one can live in the past with its disappointments, heartbreak, pain, or even the miraculous moments—for it does not exist!

The future doesn't exist, either. All we have is the moment; but moment by moment can be filled with excitement, filled with the light of peace and joy, and that kind of thinking will bring peace and joy into the future. We don't know it yet, just as the child in your old hometown didn't know all of the experiences that were to come.

It sounds complicated, but it's really the simplest idea: find things that make you happy in every moment. Train your mind to stay in the present, and when you do use your mind, use it for telling the story of the life you want. Write it down as a new story, the story you want to experience. Fill your life with moments of light, and find things to feel good about, no matter your current circumstances.

Moment by moment lived in light. What else could possibly be more important?

WINDOWS
OF HEAVEN
MEDITATION

Sit quietly, clearing your mind.

Ask God to take you to a place of peace and love
and to dissolve any thoughts of fear or anxiety.

Envision a huge window above you—
the type that opens outward with two
panes. Ask God to open these windows
to let love pour down upon you.

Suddenly the windows open and a deluge of
gold light pours down upon you. Sit and let it
flow over you. Imagine the golden light to be
like sparkling champagne, light and effervescent.
Take it in and fill up your entire body.

As it fills up the world around you, you can rise up
and move through it joyously. As you feel yourself
getting lighter and lighter, you realize the golden
sphere in your heart center is glowing brighter and
brighter until your body dissolves and the gold
light that is your essence remains, glowing brightly.

You know this light is connected to every
soul that ever was or ever will be. Enjoy
the feeling this freedom and joy brings.

Slowly open your eyes. Praise and thank God.

RESOLVING RESENTMENT

As humans, we must learn to navigate the difficulties of a split mind.

I believe we can experience only two emotions: love and fear. They may come clothed in a myriad of different ways, but it all comes down to love and fear, and if you pay attention to your body, you'll know the difference.

Fear makes you tense, your pulse quickens, a tightening in the chest may occur, and there's often a feeling of shutting down or darkness. Love opens. There's a lightness, a feeling of joy, of hope; love makes us feel whole, healed. Fear is of the ego. Love is of God, or our true selves, and therein lies the split and where the healing work is to be done.

When speaking or writing of God, everyone experiences the concept in a different way. Since my experience will be perhaps vastly different from yours, please bear with me in the language I use for my experience.

God is love, and the more God you can bring into your life, the less fear there will be. Eventually you will wake up to the knowledge that truly through God, or love, you can do all things.

It's easy to write that. The reality is much, much harder, but will be the most important work you will ever do. In the past I've written about resentment in a few forms; a friend may have snubbed me, or a server may not have brought me exactly what I ordered in a restaurant. The incidents go on and on because I allow them to. I'm now giving this up to God for healing. If I resent anyone, it means I perceive a difference between me and him or her, and to perceive a difference means that I don't see them as my brother or sister in God.

Let me give an example. Back when Damien and I were promoting our book *Yours for Eternity*, we were invited to appear on a live nighttime talk show. We had gone on that very show several times before. The host was always a gentleman to us and had a real interest in justice, the death penalty, and the state of our legal system. He had since left the show, but we agreed to go on, thinking the producers would follow in the same manner as before.

Upon arriving in the green room, we learned very quickly what we were in for. On the screen, the preview for our interview was a montage of serial killers and the women who had married them, with screams playing in the background. The host was rude, mean, and tried his best to humiliate Damien and me. I couldn't find my voice and faltered in the immediacy of the attack. The interview was a failure, and the host was gleeful that he had taken us down.

For a long time I obsessed over this man. I fantasized about all the things I wished I'd said to him. I wished for his career to end. I wanted him to be bullied as he had bullied us.

It was only recently that I realized the longer I held onto my bitterness toward him, the more I tied myself to him. I had connected myself to him with a tie stronger than steel.

The only way I know to cancel out that kind of resentment is to cast it on the Christ within me, the light within me. And to accomplish this, every time I think of that day and that man, I turn it to love. I'll start for a moment, reminded of old wounds, but then I quickly move away into feeling love for him—genuine love, for if I hate him, I hate myself. We are all connected by the only thing that never changes—God.

This is an in-the-moment practice that must be done over and over. It's difficult, but in time you'll see the hate, bitterness, and fear will slowly dissolve, and the results are nothing short of freedom.

INNER
KNOWING

A friend asked me about a difficult decision she had to make that required her loyalty. I've taken some time since to consider what loyalty means to me. I have come to understand that guilt should never come into it. Loyalty should never be won from guilt.

How often do we make decisions out of guilt? It's difficult because often our loyalty comes from someone helping us in some way, or perhaps loving and caring for us.

There's a scene in *Guess Who's Coming to Dinner* when the character played by Sidney Poitier is speaking to his father. After being berated by his dad, who expects his son to live up to his ideals because of the sacrifices he and his mother had made, the son responds that he owes his father nothing—it was his job as a father to make sacrifices for his son, and he will in turn do the same for his own children.

That's a bitter pill for most. I said that very thing to Damien in the hard times, that he owed me for what I did for him. I now know deep in my spirit that he owes me nothing. I did what I did for him for many reasons, but at the core, it was because I loved him. He owes me nothing, as I owe nothing to the people who have helped me.

That doesn't mean that those who have helped us, or raised us, shouldn't be honored, loved, or appreciated. But to act out of obligation and guilt when all that remains is hurt, judgment, or perhaps even a way of being that hinders your own destiny—to let someone remain in your life or to spend time with people who drag you down or, worse, inhibit your spiritual growth—is the big mistake we make over and over.

I believe loyalty, when it is true, comes from love. Love is not judgment or resentment, and it doesn't come with a sense of obligation. Choices made from love feel different from choices made from fear. It's not easy, but as you practice love, you'll come to realize a freedom from the tangled ties that bind, especially when those bonds come at a huge price.

I've been using a simple technique when it comes to making choices. In my spirit, whenever a situation occurs that requires that I make a decision, I ask God to let me see a red light or a green light. It never fails, and the color is vivid. There's no mistaking when to stop and when to go.

Try it the next time you're being asked to do something that requires your loyalty. Take a beat and see how you feel in your heart center. Flow, or go, is felt as green; love is green. Fear is glaring red, and you'll feel that too: a halting or a resistance to move.

This practice will also work in all other situations. You can use it to make big decisions or for something as simple as what to eat for breakfast. I tried this just the other day. Huge, glazed donut: RED. Egg-white spinach omelet: GREEN. It works every time, for any choice that needs to be made.

SOFTEN
YOUR EYES TO
CENTER IN LOVE

I used to think the person I loved would somehow "fix" me. I have learned that not only could he not fix me, but that I would set out to destroy him if he didn't. When I turned a spiritual light upon all of my delusions about what love was supposed to be, I found that each one of my relationships was a set-up for me to attack my partner.

I finally turned my relationship with Damien over to God. It was one of the scariest things I've ever done. I was at rock bottom and I really had no other choice, but I didn't know that at the time. As it worked out, as we turned our gaze to everything spiritual, our relationship healed. Our work and our life together is now focused on serving God, not the ego, and the peace and love that has resulted is beyond my wildest dreams.

We can give our relationship with the world over to God, too. I find that when out in public, I'll often harden my eyes in an effort to armor up. Now I remind myself to soften my eyes when looking out at the world.

Try this and notice how you become softer all over and no longer feel the need to attack. Do it any time you think of it. Relax your gaze and look at the world around you as you would a flower or a sunset.

FEATHERS

I don't remember when I first heard about this or from whom, but when out walking, if I see a feather on the ground, I am immediately reminded that angels are around. Sometimes it'll remind me of a particular angel with whom I'm working, bringing that energy right into the forefront of my attention.

The same can be done with any object you find yourself seeing repeatedly. I have a friend who finds playing cards on the street. You might find your attention drawn to many mundane objects—pennies, even a bit of red string can bring the attention back to the Now or bring you into a state of gratitude.

It's a lovely way to extend your spiritual practice into your daily excursions.

SEE PEOPLE AS LIGHT

This is a favorite in-the-moment ritual for when you are out walking or in any public place.

Look out at everyone you meet and see their bodies dissolve until only the golden light at their heart center is left.

See yourself as a ball of golden light—only the spirit.

See everyone as yourself, a golden light walking through the world. Only then can you see we really are all one thing. Love.

PART 4

SHIELDING &
PROTECTION

One of the things I love most about NYC is the constant ambient energy produced by all the people, movement, and activity. It is a nonstop cataclysm of psychic bombardment.

Far from being unpleasant, I now find it difficult to function without it. Anything less than the tidal waves of energy makes me feel as if I'm stagnating.

But that's not true for everyone, and sometimes I still find myself overwhelmed by the energy in densely populated areas. At those times I use the same methods I used to shield myself in prison.

To shield is to create an energetic boundary. There is a variety of reasons to become proficient at constructing these energetic barriers.

People's emotions and thoughts leave a kind of imprint upon the energy they are emitting into their environment. Some of it may be pleasant, while some of it may be outright detrimental. For example, the people at a carnival or amusement park are probably feeling emotions like excitement, happiness, and joy, whereas people in a prison yard are generating energy of a variety much lower on the vibrational spectrum: fear, rage, hatred, or outright incoherent insanity. When we absorb the energy in these situations, it affects us like secondhand smoke. For example, think of how when one person in a group panics and bolts for the door others will follow suit even before they have any idea what it is that started the panic in the first place.

We can take on the harmful or negative energies from other people, places, and things. Shielding is a way to protect yourself from their harmful effects. If you are at all empathic, shields can help prevent you from being overwhelmed by the energy you find yourself bombarded with.

We talked about cutting energetic cords in Part 2. A cord can form if you think about someone a lot, or if they are thinking about you. If someone is jealous of your success, for example, it may form an energy cord that could undermine your accomplishment. Shields can prevent these cords from forming.

Shielding rituals are adaptable and can be used in innumerable ways. Once you get good at perceiving harmful energy, a shield becomes a fast way to protect yourself. You can also use a shielding ritual as a daily preventative and protection. The more energy you put into these rituals, the stronger your shield will be.

Like all energy work, a shield is not permanent and has to be reinforced from time to time. Think of it like charging your phone. You can't just charge it once and expect it to continue working forever. All energy is eventually depleted in the physical world, and this is mirrored in the astral realm. Just as your phone has to be recharged, so too must your shield.

Remember that, like all other acts of magick we perform, we never use our own energy when creating a shield. That would eventually lead to depletion. Instead, we take in energy from the world around us through our breath.

Finally, these sorts of shielding techniques aren't limited to self-use. You can use them to shield a room, your house, an entire apartment building—or once you become proficient enough, your whole block. You can place shields around objects such as journals, magickal tools, or other people. I have included shielding rituals in this section that

you can adapt to just about any purpose you can think of—
even a shield that only lets love in.

SPHERE OF LIGHT SHIELD

Energy is incredibly contagious. We are taking in and absorbing energy all the time—some of which may not be beneficial. For example, if you spend a great deal of time around people who constantly criticize others, you may find yourself soon doing the same thing.

Everyone knows someone who can't see anything but the negative. It's like they approach each and every situation almost as if they are looking for something to complain about.

The same goes for anger—some people walk through life looking for things to take offense at. Spend much time around these people, and you'll find yourself becoming as miserable and angry as they are.

I thought about this a great deal when I was in prison; about how we absorb energy from people around us.

The thought of beginning to resemble the energy I was surrounded by was horrifying, so I constantly took measures to protect myself.

When magicians perform large rituals, they're attempting to accumulate as much of a particular kind of energy into an area as possible. The first step in such a ritual is what is called casting a circle. When we do this, we're usually drawing a circle of light around the area where we're doing the ritual. When constructing a shield, we do the same thing, except we're drawing the circle around ourselves so that it moves with us throughout the day. This ritual is a greatly simplified version of a circle of invocation and was one of the things I did daily in prison. Of the shielding rituals, it is my personal favorite due to how effective I've found it to be:

I close my eyes and take several
deep and even breaths.

As I inhale, I visualize myself pulling in energy
from the world around me. I envision it as white
light, which passes through my body and into
the earth beneath my feet. With every inhalation,
the earth is filled with more and more bright
light until, by the tenth breath, it's completely
filled with as much brilliant light as possible.

After about ten inhalations, I stretch my right arm out before me, with the first two fingers of my hand extended and the last two fingers folded into my palm with my thumb over them. In magick this is called the sword mudra because it can be used to sever energy. It is also used for directing energy.

I begin to turn in a circle while envisioning
the light within the earth rushing back up
through my body, out of my pointing fingers.
I use it to draw a circle of white light around
myself. I imagine it looking like a hula hoop
made of light, surrounding my body at slightly
lower than chest level. I make sure to end
where I began, so that the circle is complete.

I then stretch both arms out to my sides with
palms up and "grasp" the ring of light. I slowly
raise my arms up above my head while visualizing
that I'm stretching the light and closing it above
me like a dome. Then I stretch my arms out to
my sides again with palms facing down and
stretch the energy to close it beneath my feet.

I am now standing inside a brilliant egg-
shaped sphere of white light. I sometimes
even feel a kind of energetic "pop" as I close
the sphere around myself. This is caused
by the sudden severing or separating from
the energetic field we exist within.

When you first begin this practice, you'll have to reinforce the shield a few times a day. The more accustomed you grow to doing it and the stronger your ability becomes, the longer and more effectively it will stay in place.

AURA SHIELD

The more time you spend walking the path of magick, the more ways you tend to find of doing a particular thing—kind of like that old saying, "There's more than one way to skin a cat." We would never skin our cats. It's just a saying! But there are countless ways that an energetic shield can be constructed. I'm going to give a couple more examples that will perhaps inspire you to experiment and come up with your own method if you're so inclined.

The first variation on the shielding technique utilizes your heart center and your aura.

Imagine a gold sphere of light in
the center of your chest.

Begin taking slow, even breaths, seeing the
sphere glow brighter and brighter with every
inhalation as you fill it with more energy.

After breathing deeply at least three times (I
myself prefer to do it ten times), exhale and see
the golden energy you've accumulated spread out
like a ripple in all directions through your aura,
until it reaches the very outer perimeter—about
an arm's length around you in every direction.

As you see it spread through your aura, know that it
is patching and repairing any damage that you may
have accumulated. It reinforces the outer perimeter
of your aura, giving it a pliable yet tough boundary—
slightly rubbery, and capable of bouncing any
energy directed at you back to its source.

I recommend repeating this process three
times, following it by grounding out any
excess energy into the earth with one of
the visualization techniques from Part 2.

POWER
SHIELD

This shielding ritual is a little more advanced than the previous two. This takes some practice to get used to but can feel incredibly powerful once you've mastered it.

Begin by standing in the center of your
ritual space, inhaling the energy that
permeates the world around you. It passes
through your body, out your feet, and fills
the earth with brilliant white light.

With every inhalation, the light within
the earth grows brighter and brighter.

After doing this from three to ten times,
step forward with your left foot as you exhale,
and extend both arms before you while
allowing the energy to rush back up through
your body and toward your hands.

Now eject the energy from your hands. See it being flung all the way to the very edge of the universe, where it bounces back toward you with tremendously increased velocity. When it slams back into you, the light wraps around you and completely envelops you in an egg-shaped dome.

SHIELDING TO LET LOVE IN

S ome people prefer not to block out all energy with a solid shield. If they're empathic, they often feel like it cuts them off from being able to "read" the energy of a person or place. People who have a keenly developed perception of energy can feel like they are in a stale vacuum if they shield themselves so that no energy at all can penetrate. Others may want to absorb some of the more beneficial energies within a location, while filtering out more detrimental "flavors" of energy.

Whatever the reason, you may want to create a less dense or solid sort of shield that is programmed with an intention to allow certain energy in but still hold others out. You do this in the same way you create the solid shield, but with some variations.

This variation on the Sphere of Light ritual creates a shield that only higher, love-based energies can enter. We do it exactly the same way we did with the Sphere of Light shielding exercise, only we do it while visualizing the circle being drawn with pink light, since pink is one of the colors associated with the planet of Venus. In the magickal tradition we say that Venus is the heavenly body that corresponds with the energy of love.

Begin by inhaling several times—at least three, but as many times as you'd like. Keep in mind that the more you do it, the more energy you're putting into the shield.

As you inhale, see light being drawn from the universe around you. It goes in through your nose, down through your body, out the soles of your feet, and into the earth. With every inhalation, the entire earth is filled with light, growing brighter and brighter.

When you feel that you've collected enough energy, extend your right hand out and using the sword mudra begin drawing a circle of pink light around you at waist level. As you do so, think to yourself, "Only higher vibrational, love-based energy can penetrate this sphere."

End as before—by extending your arms out
to your sides with your palms upturned, and
slowly raise them until your palms meet above
your head. Envision that you're pulling the
circle closed like a dome above your head.

Then do the same below, closing the circle of
pink light beneath your feet. Envision yourself
as standing inside an egg-shaped bubble
of pink light that goes wherever you go.

Inhale one final time, and as you do so,
envision the pink egg of light growing as
bright as you can possibly visualize it.

Go about your activities as usual, remembering
to perform the ritual again in a few hours.

SELECTIVE
SHIELDING

This variation of the Sphere of Light ritual can be adapted to allow in any type of desired energy, while still protecting you from negative energies.

This time, draw the ring of light with the
intention that it be porous. Envision it as either
having a spongy or smoke-like texture. Instead
of reflecting energy back toward its source
or out into the universe, it will ABSORB all
the energy you come into contact with.

As you close the light dome above your head and
below your feet, know that as it absorbs energy,
it only allows beneficial or clean energy to enter
your aura, while everything else gets grounded
out and into the earth in the same way that
you did it in the grounding exercises. Visualize
the unwanted energies sliding off of the aura
and going down into the earth to be recycled.

SHIELDING FOR ABUNDANCE

In this variation we're going to create a shield that only energies of prosperity and abundance can enter. Its purpose is to prevent lack or scarcity from entering our "sphere of sensation," which is just the old-fashioned term for aura.

In this version you can choose to use either green or blue light. Green is the color usually associated with the element of earth, and blue is the color associated with the planetary energy of Jupiter. Both the element of earth and the planet of Jupiter correspond with or symbolize things like wealth, abundance, prosperity, and expansion.

Whichever you choose depends entirely upon which you favor. Personally, I have sometimes used both at the same time. In that case I surround myself with one shield of green light for earth and then another shield of blue around that, so that I have layered two shields, one over the other.

Begin by practicing the breathing exercise, inhaling light from the universe around you. It enters through your nose, passes through your body, out the soles of your feet, and into the earth beneath you.

With every inhalation the earth fills with more and more brilliant light. Then stretch out your right arm and, using the sword mudra (extending the first and middle finger), begin to slowly turn in a circle while drawing a line of green light in the air around you.

When you arrive back facing the way you began, hold both arms out to your sides with the palms up. Slowly bring both arms up over your head until your palms touch, envisioning that you are stretching the circle—closing it over your head like a green dome. Then do the same thing in a downward motion, envisioning that you are closing the green circle beneath your feet. While doing so, say to yourself, "Only energies of prosperity and abundance may enter this shield."

Inhale once more, seeing the green egg of light
around you grow as bright as you can make it.

Next you can repeat the process—if you desire
to do so—by beginning to inhale energy into
the earth and using it to draw a circle of blue
light OUTSIDE the green egg-shield.

Go through the motions of closing it
above and below you, so that the green
earth shield is now inside the blue Jupiter
shield. Again, say to yourself, "Only
prosperity and abundance may enter."

See yourself enclosed in the blue shield, and see it
grow as bright as possible as you inhale once more.

Go about your day, remembering to
reinforce the shields after a few hours.

QUICK RITUAL FOR A PRIVATE CONVERSATION IN PUBLIC SPACE

I live in a city, immersed in a sea of humanity at all times. I love the din of sound and energy this creates, but sometimes you just want to have a private conversation somewhere like a crowded restaurant or coffee shop. This ritual makes that possible. It is one of the absolute easiest acts of magick you can perform, and it's also a perfect example of how to use magick in daily life.

You can do this as an "empty hand technique"—meaning we use nothing but our own ingenuity and the energy we draw from the universe around us—or we can incorporate a component of natural magick to boost its effects. In this case, the component that adds the extra kick is nothing more than table salt.

Throughout recorded history, magicians have used salt for protecting themselves, others, or the space where they're doing magick from outside energies of all kinds. Salt is basically millions of tiny crystals that can be held in the palm of your hand.

First, just take the saltshaker and sprinkle a pinch of it in the center of your table.

Then close your eyes and begin to take slow, steady inhalations. With each indrawn breath, envision that you are drawing in energy from the universe around you in the form of white light. It passes through your body and into the earth. As you exhale, know that the air may be leaving your lungs, but the energy remains in the earth.

Focus on building that energy as powerfully as you can, seeing the earth fill with more light with each indrawn breath. When you feel like you've accumulated enough energy, use the first finger on your right hand to draw the rune known as "Berkano" in white light at the center of the salt crystals.

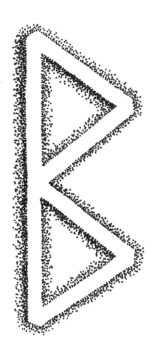

Berkano is most commonly known for
its connection to things like growth
and rebirth—but it also corresponds
to things like secrecy and privacy.

As you draw the rune in light, hold the intent
that you're doing it to shield your table from the
world around you—closing out the energy of
other people who surround you, and giving you
the privacy needed to carry out your business
without notice. You'll discover that those
around you take no note of your conversation.

SHIELD FOR INVISIBILITY

This invisibility ritual was incredibly useful in a prison environment, where you don't want to attract any more notice than you absolutely have to. I learned this technique from reading John Michael Greer's books. By invisibility I do not mean that you will literally vanish and become transparent to anyone looking at you. It's more like a kind of camouflage that allows you to blend into the world, so that people take no notice of you unless they are looking specifically for you. After working with it for a while, I simplified it even further by eliminating the use of tools and the ceremonial format. While nowhere near as eloquent as John Michael Greer's ritual, I found that my own version provided more than adequate results.

It essentially works exactly the same as the previous shielding techniques where you enclose yourself in an egg-shaped bubble of light, but this time we visualize it as being a deep, inky black (black being the color associated with the planet Saturn).

Begin by inhaling several times—at least three, but more if you want to make the effect stronger or last longer. Remember that the more effort you put into it, the more effect you're likely to get out of it.

With each inhalation you are drawing chi, or energy, from the world around you.

Visualize it as if you are inhaling light that passes through your body, out the soles of your feet, and into the earth. See every inhalation completely filling the earth with light.

When you feel that you've accumulated enough chi/energy, extend your right arm and use the sword mudra to begin drawing a line of black light around yourself as you slowly turn in a circle. Begin back where you started so that you have connected the circle.

Reaching both arms out to your sides with
both palms facing up, slowly raise them above
your head until your palms touch. As you
do so, envision that you are stretching the
circle, closing it above your head like a dome.
Repeat this movement with palms facing
downward, envisioning that you are stretching
the circle to close it beneath your feet.

Take a moment to visualize yourself completely
enclosed in a black sphere, and KNOW
that the eyes of anyone not looking for you
specifically will glide over you while taking
little to no interest in you or your activities.

The effect will wear off after a few hours—the time will
vary depending on how much energy you put into it and
how adept you become at it.

PROTECTING AN OBJECT

There are many ways to use the energy of Saturn for protection. For example, if you want to protect an object from the eyes of others, say, your diary or magickal journal, bring down black light upon it. It's possible to bring light down on objects and people who are not in your vicinity—the magick works just as effectively when done remotely. One of the more creative uses I've heard of was a friend telling me that they constructed a shield around their computer to protect their social media accounts and keep them hidden from the eyes of "haters."

Hold the object in your hands or
imagine holding it in your hands.

Breathe deeply ten times, letting the
breath fill you with light and energy
that you send down into the earth.

Draw energy up from the center of
the earth to form a black ball around
the object you are holding.

KNOW that this shield protects the
object from any unwanted attention.

PART 5

DIRECTING, PROJECTING & CHARGING

One of the most practical and exciting forms of energy work is projecting and directing. I've always favored energy-directing rituals and techniques over passive kinds of meditation such as zazen or mindfulness. Part of the reason was that I saw such powerful results from working with energy—and in a drastically shorter period of time than anything I experienced from meditation.

The more thought, preparation, concentration, and effort that you put into a ritual, the more energy you are generating. That energy can then be directed toward different purposes. When doing this work, you are acting on the etheric or astral level of reality—this creates a blueprint from which the physical world is shaped and created.

There are two ways to project and direct energy: Pull energy into yourself and project it outwards, or pull energy down onto objects, places, or people outside of yourself. It bears repeating that in magick, we never use our own energy. To do so would deplete us. Drawing energy from outside sources and then directing it outwards to accomplish something is what enables us to create our own worlds.

This section also includes rituals to charge substances and objects for use in magick. I haven't always been a big fan of using material "props" like wands in my rituals. This is because in prison I had to learn what one of my teachers, a woman named Dorothy Morrison, called the "empty hand technique." She called it this because I had absolutely nothing material to use—no candles, no incense, no tools. Just myself. It made me realize that all of those things are essentially just training wheels. They are props that help us eventually learn to do magick anytime and anywhere, with no sort of external dependency. Using tools in magick can therefore be a liability if you feel you can ONLY do magick when you have them, but it also does something else. It allows you to create a powerful artifact that adds its ever-increasing strength to whatever intention you're trying to realize.

BOLTS
OF LIGHT

This section of the book is Damien's area of expertise, but there is a very specific ritual for directing energy that I sometimes do several times a day. As with so many of our rituals, I breathe in enormous amounts of golden light, turning my entire being into a ball of light resembling the sun. I then take that concentrated energy and imagine it flowing out to people close to me who are in need of help or healing.

The energy I send is programmed with love, joy, healing, protection, strength, prosperity, creativity, inspiration, healing, and wisdom. Everything is divinely orchestrated. It's clear that none of this comes from me, but through me from God.

A few of the people to which I have sent gold light have been in dire situations. Some of them have played huge parts in my and Damien's lives, but have become distant, or at times cut off. We never take these lapses personally, knowing when any of us are in pain, we tend to go inward or seek cover.

Several of these people have since reached out to me. Some have asked for help, and I've prayed for guidance as to how to best assist or direct them. The right path has always been clear or has wondrously appeared. Some have provided support to Damien and me, and others have had epiphanies or huge changes occur that have propelled them to a new understanding or situation that brings them peace or joy.

As happens often, the results of this ritual have been under my radar. Knowing that magick ALWAYS works, I'm also practicing releasing expectations, so I don't always realize when a prayer works. It's exhilarating when we realize just how amazingly it does.

When Damien was on death row, I'd have kind-hearted people tell me they'd put us on their prayer lists. I'm certain there were many more I didn't hear from who also did so. I believe all of those prayers helped in the huge amount of energy that was needed to facilitate his release, and now, more than ever, I'm grateful to all of those who prayed for us.

My "prayer list" is growing, as it's one of the most satisfying rituals of my spiritual practice. It is God working through me, and while I know the inspiration for change isn't coming from me, knowing that I can direct the energy to those in need brings much joy, in many ways.

You can also do this practice at the moment you notice someone in need. We can all have bad days. I do this tiny ritual when someone I come across seems to be having a hard time of it:

> I imagine a bright golden light above me,
> and I breathe in from that light, filling my
> heart chakra. I then very quickly exhale and
> shoot golden light into the troubled person.

> If I only have a moment, they may only
> get that one bolt, but often I'll continue
> sending as many bolts as I can, hoping
> within a few moments they'll feel relief.

A note: In some traditions, to heal someone or to send energy without their consent is considered disrespectful. I grew up praying for people whether they knew about it or not. Our church had prayer lists. There would be folks from all over the world on the list, and we prayed for everyone on the planet. I'm following in this tradition of sending energy to others, but if you feel uncomfortable helping anyone without their consent, the energy can be programmed to go only where it is wanted and needed.

CHARGING A
GLASS OF WATER

We begin the practice of sending and re-
ceiving energy with the hands because
there are large energy centers in the
palms that facilitate it. In fact, there are energy centers
all over the body. Most people are familiar with the
seven energy centers we call the chakras. Many people
in Western practices like High Magick and Kabbalah
are familiar with the five energy centers used in these
traditions. However, there are actually about 360 total
energy centers in the body, all joined and connected
by pathways that acupuncturists call meridians. The
reason we feel drawn to hold hands with those we love
is that we want to exchange energy. The same goes for
kissing. The hands are a vehicle for directing energy.
Think of Reiki, or the laying of hands on the Bible.

Even looking at someone can create a huge surge of directed energy. Think of that the next time you meet a loved one's eyes across the room.

There are many ways to direct energy to charge a substance or an object, but here is one of the easiest methods.

Place a glass of water on a table or counter before you. Inhale three times while visualizing the earth filling with more and more white light beneath your feet.

Envision the entire earth filling with more and more white light every time you inhale.

Visualize the air you inhale as white light that you are inhaling from the universe around you. This white light goes through your nostrils, through your body, and out through the soles of your feet and into the earth.

The entire earth is filled with this glowing white light—more and more of it, growing brighter and brighter with every inhalation.

Each time you exhale, visualize that the air is
being released, but the chi stays within the
earth until you consciously choose to release it.

When you are ready to release it, visualize
all of the white light rushing back up
through your body as you exhale, down your
right arm, and out of your right hand.

Hold your right hand over the water—or hold
the glass in your hand. As you exhale, see the
light rush up through your body, out of your hand,
and into the water. See the water in your mind's
eye as being filled with brilliant white light.

As you drink the water, visualize the
light spreading through your entire
body, filling it with light.

You should practice this with a glass of water several
times a day until you are proficient at it. Once mastered,
it can be utilized for many different purposes.

BLESSING FOOD

This exercise is a variation on the Glass of Water ritual. Often in magick when we learn a single ritual or technique, what we're actually doing is learning a formula that can be used in a variety of different ways. Traditionally, these variations were never taught— you were expected to figure them out for yourself.

What we will do now is use energy to draw patterns that carry an intent. In this case our intent will be to bless our food.

In modern times we often gobble our food absentmind- edly while multitasking—watching television, talking with friends, or working on the computer. Blessing our food not only imbues it with more chi, or energy, but it also reminds us to come back to the present moment and remember that everything we do is a step toward com- pleting the Great Work.

Begin by inhaling several times while visualizing
the chi being drawn through your nose, down
through your body, and out through your feet. It
fills the earth with white light. The white light
grows brighter and brighter with each inhalation.

Then, extend your right hand out over your
food, and as the light/energy rushes back up
through your body and out your hand, use your
first and second fingers to surround your food
in flaming blue light, the color of the flames
that come from the burner on a gas stove.

As you eat your meal, visualize each
mouthful of food as being infused with
the divine light, and see it spread out
through your entire body as you swallow.

DIRECTING ENERGY FOR PAIN RELIEF

One of the ways I used directed energy on myself in prison was to relieve pain. I'd put both hands on whatever body part was hurting, and then spend several minutes just focusing on breathing chi into my chest when I inhaled. You can probably guess what comes next! If you try this on yourself, cultivate your chi through the breath and visualization. Then, on the exhale, see it move from your chest, down your arms, out of your hands, and into the body part. With every exhalation, the body part glows brighter and brighter gold, more and more filled with energy.

I did this often to help with the pain in my teeth. The relief from pain allowed me to hang on until I was released.

CHARGING
A CANDLE

Nearly everyone loves incorporating candles into ritual work, because something about them has always been synonymous with magick. We can put energy into them by drawing in light from the world around us with our breath. We can then access that energy when we ritually burn the candle. They serve as batteries to hold energy.

In addition to the energy you yourself put into the candle, there is also energy from two other sources. First you must take the energy of the color of the candle into consideration. Each color is a different portion of the light spectrum and vibrates at a different frequency. Red, for example, is much more active than earthy colors like brown. And blue is from the slower, calmer part of the light spectrum. You can choose which kinds of energy you want to add to your ritual by which color candle you use. Below are a few of the many traditional color correspondences in magick, but you should feel free to experiment. Colors may have specific and unique associations to you and these will have an effect on your work. If a color feels right to you, then chances are that's the one you should go with.

The color correspondences here are not carved in stone and are intended to be guidelines for you to expand upon. Your own experiments and intuition will help you discover what is most beneficial to your practice. The following is a short list I put together after several years of practice, and which I've found to be beneficial. See page 234 for further color correspondences.

- **RED**: Protection, adding force to ritual, romance

- **ORANGE**: Speed, all business matters, communication

- **YELLOW**: Victory and success, balance and harmony, general healing

- **GREEN**: Grounding, prosperity, strength

- **BLUE**: Abundance, growth, expansion

- **VIOLET**: Enhancing psychic intuition, lucid dreaming, anything moon-related

- **BLACK**: Banishing, binding harmful energy, anything related to time or karma

- **WHITE**: When in doubt use white as it contains all the colors, general blessing

Lastly, there is the actual fire from the burning candle. The fire generates heat and energy as it transmutes the candle from a solid to a liquid. When you burn your charged candle, you can visualize the flame itself powering your intention.

As you inhale, visualize the golden energy center in your chest growing as bright as possible due to the energy you're pulling in.

As you exhale, visualize that light traveling from the gold sphere in your chest down your arms, out the palms of your hands, and into the candle.

Repeat this part of the ritual every day for
several days. Spend perhaps ten minutes
a day at the same time each day for three
days pushing energy into the candle.

On the third day, light the candle
and let it burn down.

This can be done repeatedly, with more and more energy being put into the candle. You could do it for seven days, or even a month before you burn the candle. There is no time limit. If what you're trying to manifest is a good parking spot, it won't take nearly as much time and energy as a new house for your family to live in.

CHARGING WITH
THE FULL MOON

I have always been drawn to mudras, and I use them regularly. Mudras are particular hand gestures that make connections between two or more energy centers. Some are deeply symbolic and rely on the power of the symbolism more than on the energy centers being connected.

Take the "live long and prosper" sign used by Leonard Nimoy in *Star Trek*. This is a traditional mudra used by Jewish priests to bestow a blessing and is symbolic of the astrological sign of Aries. The gesture, which is made by spreading the ring and middle fingers apart to make a "v" shape, represents the ram's foot.

A favorite way of "pulling down energy" to charge an item is with a mudra called the "Triangle of Manifestation." It's performed by holding both of your hands out before

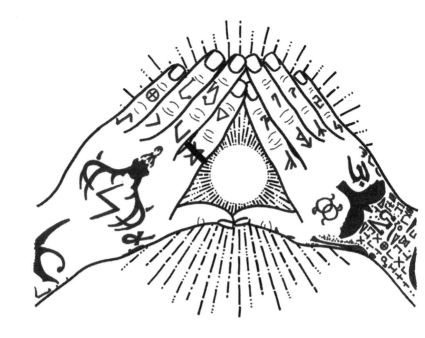

you, palms outward. Touch the tips of your thumbs together, as well as the tips of your first fingers. The space left in between your hands should look like a triangle.

In his book *Modern Magick*, Donald Michael Kraig describes a technique to charge a talisman using this mudra. A talisman is any object charged with the intention of bringing something to you. Kraig says you'll know it's successful when you feel a sensation that something has clicked into place. I kept trying and trying to do it and never felt that signal of success until I added some additional energy to it. What follows is my adaptation of his method that combines the triangle of manifestation mudra with the technique of charging an item by holding it between your palms. The purpose for this is two-fold: to add even more power to your working, and to encourage you to continue constantly experimenting so that you find new methods that not only work for you, but that you also enjoy doing.

Stand outside so that you can see the full moon.

Have the object or substance that
you want to charge before you.

Hold your hands up so that you are
looking at the moon through the center
of the Triangle of Manifestation.

Bring your hands down, without breaking
the triangle, and place them over whatever
you are charging so that the object, herbs,
etc., is between your hands and inside
the Triangle of Manifestation.

The trick to making this method work is
visualizing the moon. As you lower your
hands down over whatever you're charging,
the moon's image remains within the triangle,
as if you are taking it out of the nighttime
sky and putting it inside the object.

After you lower the Triangle of Manifestation over the object you are charging, shift your focus to the golden orb of energy in the center of your chest. Inhale three times, seeing it glow brighter and brighter gold as it is filled with energy.

As you exhale between inhalations, visualize that you are releasing the air, but the energy stays inside.

After the third inhalation, as you exhale see all of the energy rush from the energy center in your chest, down your arms, out your hands, and into the object.

Close the ritual by knocking lightly on the table or altar where you are doing magick three times and visualize it sealing the energy into the item.

RITUAL
OBJECTS

When magicians talk about consecrating an item, what we're describing is imbuing an item with divine energy to bless it. When this is done repeatedly with an object, you create a kind of holy artifact due to the way energy accumulates over time.

Novice magicians are told to, whenever possible, do their rituals in the same place each day. The reason for this is that energy gradually accumulates there, enhancing any magick done in the space. This is also true of all the tools and paraphernalia used during rituals. The more we use our tools, the more of a "charge" they build—making all magick done with them even more effective. This is the same reason that magicians traditionally had an article of clothing that was worn during ritual work—so that every time you do magick while wearing it, it absorbs a little more energy that will aid and assist with future endeavors.

The wand is the preeminent tool of magick. In fact, when most think of a magician, one of the first associations that comes to mind is the wand. This has been true since the dawn of human civilization, where we find wands used for various purposes in traditions from the ancient Sumerian magi to the Old Testament prophets. In Christian iconography, the earliest depictions of Jesus ever created show him using a wand to call Lazarus forth from his tomb. In many Sumerian carvings you will see the king or one of the gods holding what is referred to as a rod and ring. This was passed to the king by the deities, representing his divine right to rule. It showed that he had been found worthy of the position by Divinity itself.

The ring or circle represented eternity because it had no beginning or end—just like the gods themselves. The rod represents the finite lifespan of the king, showing that his life—and rulership—has both a beginning and an end. The rod would be symbolically wielded by both the king, in the form of a scepter, and the priests, in the form of a wand. This is the origin of the magician's wand.

In magick the wand symbolizes the element of fire and an extension of the will of the one who wields it. In his book *Modern Magick*, Donald Michael Kraig goes so far as to say that the magician should sleep with the wand in bed with them for a month, so that it is continuously bathed in their energy field, which makes it even more connected to them. When not being used, the wand is wrapped in a black cloth to protect it from outside energies, and it shouldn't be handled by others.

The history, use, and correspondences of wands is an entire field of study unto itself. Some traditions, such as the Golden Dawn, use multiple wands for different purposes. Neophytes usually began by using a wand that looked like a small wooden rod, with one end painted black and one end painted white. The white end was for basic, minor invoking, the black end for banishing.

Wands can be made of particular woods, metals, and stones so that the energies are woven into the magick done with them. For example, if you want to make a wand to use only in rituals that deal with love in some way, it could be made of the wood of an apple tree, since apple trees correspond with Venus. Woods that correspond with the planetary energy of Jupiter—such as oak—are traditional for wands used in rituals for any kind of prosperity, expansion, or wisdom. A wand made specifically for protection or defensive rituals, including things like warding your home, could be made of ash, which corresponds with the energy of Mars.

While some magicians may go so far as to have a different wand for each of the energies they work with, others use a single wand for all work. This is what I do, for the most part, although I also have one I take on the road with me because I don't want to chance something happening to my main one. If I have to travel, taking my wand with me on the road is like taking a piece of my temple with me. It's topped with a quartz crystal, because quartz holds energy better than just about any other material.

Some will swear that all your tools—including a wand—should be made by you. That is certainly a route you can go. However, I made neither of mine. They are both one of a kind, handcrafted by a wandmaker in Colorado. My main wand is made from the found leg bone of a deer, a piece of oak, and the finial from an antique chair. There's an old cliche saying, "When the student is ready, the teacher will appear." Sometimes magickal tools are the same. The one that you're supposed to have just seems to find its way to you.

The most common magician's tools, other than the wand, are the chalice, pentacle, athame (or ritual blade), and robe. Do not go out and try to obtain all of your tools at once. You'll be tempted to do this, but it's much more powerful to collect them one at a time, with great deliberation and attentiveness. Make the project of collecting your tools a ritual unto itself. Wait and see what will call out to you, or what you'll be drawn to.

Begin by doing a magick ritual to obtain a wand. To start, visualize your wand, and bring gold light down upon it, asking that you find the perfect tool to aid you in accomplishing the Great Work within this lifetime. Then let go of the outcome and let the magick do its work.

Once your wand finds its way to you, you can then do the same ritual for a chalice, pentacle, athame, robe, or any magickal tool.

You'll find through the years that you will have collected things that are incredibly personal to you but may not even remotely resemble the items depicted in traditional grimoires. That's as it should be, as your tools serve as an extension of yourself—and every magician is unique unto themselves.

RITUAL
SUBSTANCES

I travel a lot. In fact, there have been long stretches of time since my release that we practically lived on the road. Even when I'm home in NYC, I'm still constantly moving from place to place. When you spend a great deal of your time on the move, you don't always have the time, ability, or location to do an extended ritual—which can limit the amount of energy you're able to put into your working. This limitation can be compensated for if you plan ahead of time. A mage with enough preparation time can be a formidable thing.

My own preferred component is powders of various kinds because they are easiest and quickest to use. And when you're doing magick in public and trying not to draw strange looks, you need quick and easy. When I say "powders," I'm talking about anything from the ash from burning incense on my altar to herbs that have been dried and crushed to a fine dust. I also use salt and sand of various colors, like what Tibetan monks use when making mandalas.

Salt is one of the substances that has been used in protection rituals since the dawn of human civilization— probably due at least in part to the fact that salt is just millions of tiny crystals. Salt works by absorbing negative energy and trapping it, which is where the old tradition of throwing a pinch of salt over your shoulder to avert evil comes from. I carry a small, glass, cork-topped vial filled with blessed sea salt with me when I'm out and about. I place it on my altar each day as I'm doing my rituals, and it stays there each day accumulating more and more energy. Sometimes I've let the energy build for months before using it.

When I do take it out, I use it in places that are sacred to me in some way or serve as personal places of power, places I want to surround and encircle with protective energy in order to create holy ground. Doing this can also serve to form a kind of magickal link between yourself and the place, so that any magick you do there will be enhanced. The location itself can be just about anywhere. One of my sacred spots is a small park tucked away behind some buildings on the island of Manhattan. I call it a park, but that doesn't really do it justice, or conjure what it's like in your mind's eye. It's a chunk of earth, stone, and greenery that rises two stories into the air. I can stand atop it and look across the Hudson River to New Jersey. It's like a small citadel, made of old stone transported from crumbling Irish ruins, with spiked iron gates. Growing around and within it are flowers of all different colors and greenery so pure it doesn't look real. There's even a stone fireplace in the center of the monument, perfect for holding candles and incense. If I want to add as much power as possible to a ritual, this is where I go.

For a while I was obsessed with incenses like real frankincense, dragon's blood, and white copal. I burned them to the point that the neighbors even started to complain, saying it looked like a permanent misty haze permeated their apartment.

Anytime we were facing what looked like overwhelming obstacles or odds, I'd take a small jar of the incense ashes and direct energy into it while visualizing a happy outcome. I'd sprinkle those ashes on our front stoop and saw amazing results.

Despite that, my days of experimenting with incense came to an end due to respiratory difficulties. I had asthma often as a child, and nearly twenty years of repeated exposure to tear gas and pepper spray aggravated that condition.

Consecrated ashes and salt can be used for all kinds of ritual work. Here are just a few possible ritual uses:

Sprinkle over the threshold for protecting
a room or the entrance to any building.

Smudge a smear of ash on a
person to bring blessings.

To make holy water, bring white light down on a
glass of water to purify it, stir in the charged ash
or salt, and bring gold light down on it to bless it.
The holy water can then be sprinkled anywhere:
on people, on plants, or throughout rooms.

GROUP
BLESSING
RITUAL

nother variation on the technique of chan-
neling energy through the hands involves
working with others. One or more people
focus on sending energy to someone else, who then
gives it shape and intention. For example, once I did
this with two other magicians, one of whom wanted to
bless the threshold of his home. I gave him a small vial
of ash from my altar, which I had collected by burning
frankincense resin. Before using it, he held it between
his palms while I stood on one side of him and the
other magician stood on the opposite side. Both of us
put one hand on his chest and one on his back, so that
his energy center was between our palms.

We focused on breathing energy into the centers in our own chests, and then allowed it to travel down through our hands and into his chest as we exhaled. We didn't try to give it a direction, or program an intent into the energy. We just focused on sending it to him, to do with what he chose. He then focused on sending the energy directed by the three of us into the ash, with the intent of blessing and protecting his home.

There are no restrictions on the number of people that can be involved in a ritual like this. It can be done for just about any purpose. It's powerful to form a circle—a meeting of people who decide to get together once a month to help each other do work for whatever needs arise in their life. Such an act of communion and fellowship can be a ritual unto itself.

PLANT
MAGICK

At one point shortly after my release from prison I decided to try some very light alchemical work. I was staying in a massive labyrinth of a building in NYC, so I finally had plenty of room and had access to ingredients.

When I was in prison I'd fantasized and daydreamed about being able to try some of these procedures, and I always swore to myself that if I ever got out of there alive, I'd do it.

What you're doing with an alchemical procedure is taking a natural substance, such as a plant, and transforming it into a much more potent, purified form. Even if you're working with plants in this way, it's still astrological energies that you're focused on. In magick we use what are called correspondences. This is a way of categorizing by energy. This system goes back as long as human civilization does, but it's perhaps more popular now than ever thanks to the internet. You can quickly do research on your computer and have immediate access to what plants correspond to which planetary energies. The chart of correspondences on page 239 also lists some safe-to-consume plants and their related planetary energies. What appealed to me about alchemy was the potential for creating immensely powerful, portable magick.

An example would be Venus. The planetary energy of Venus is associated with sensuality, luxury, beauty, and love. By taking a plant or herb that corresponds with Venus, you can reduce it down to its purest essence or "salt" while doing associated rituals. I have not gotten that far in the operation, but I know someone who has, and I've seen the end result. The "salt" looks kind of like tiny pink crystals.

The process of creating a salt is a little complicated and possibly hazardous, especially without proper equipment and ventilation. But you can get a taste of alchemy by creating your own plant tincture. When I first did this, I settled on St. John's Wort. It corresponds with solar energy, which is associated with things like victory and success, so I figured I'd find lots of little practical reasons to use it and see what kind of results I experienced.

Along with the herb itself, I gathered a bottle of moonshine made at a distillery in Brooklyn. You can use any sort of pure alcohol that is 80-proof or better. You'll also need a glass container big enough to hold both the herbs and the bottle of alcohol that can be sealed airtight. I took the extra step of using the kind of jar with a clamp-on lid and a rubber seal between the glass top and bottom, sometimes called a French canning jar. This assured the contents would never come into contact with any sort of metal.

Once you have gathered your materials, pour the herbs into the jar, and then pour enough alcohol over them to completely submerge them. You don't want any of the plant material sticking up out of the alcohol, or else bacteria can grow on it. And since you are going to be doing this for thirty days, you may have to add a little more alcohol as time goes on. It evaporates, and you want to make sure all the herbs stay completely submerged. The plants themselves will soak up some of the alcohol.

Once you seal the top, keep the container somewhere that it will receive very little light but constant warmth. John Michael Greer's book on natural magick offers a great idea: to put it in the closet, on top of a hot water heater.

Once a day, take the jar out to perform a ritual to invoke the planetary energy associated with your plant over it. You do this just as you would charge a glass of water, but focus on the planet in question and draw energy specifically from it, sending that through your hands and into the tincture. This is a ritualistic way of putting more and more chi, or energy, into the concoction every day for a month, to enhance the plant's own naturally inherent energy.

Anytime you aren't doing this ritual, the jar goes back on the hot water heater. Heat is a form of energy, so the constant warmth is another form of energy being received by the elixir in the jar.

After the elixir has been allowed to sit for at least one month and strengthened by daily invocations, strain the plant material from the liquid. The alcohol will have turned a very dark green as it absorbed the plant's essence. That liquid in and of itself is a potent tincture that holds at least thirty days' worth of ritual work and intention. Store it in a bottle, and whenever you need to invoke the energy that corresponds with that particular planet, place a few drops of the tincture in a glass of water or directly under your tongue. It sends a little burst of that energy through your aura.

If you're trying to gain long-term benefits, use the tincture consistently. This allows the energy to accumulate within your aura. Say, for example, that you were trying to draw more love, sensuality, and pleasure into your life. Do your research to find a plant that both corresponds to Venus and isn't poisonous or allergenic. After going through the process of making the tincture, use it twice a day for a month, once in the morning and once at night.

Keep a daily journal so you can look back and see how your life gradually changed over the time period you were doing the work. Sometimes magick works in a subtle way that you don't even realize until you look back in hindsight and see how the situation eventually ended up. A journal can help you to see things in hindsight that you may have missed at the time.

A TALISMAN
TALE

Mostly my prison days seem like something that happened lifetimes ago, and they rarely cross my mind. That's all the past, and I don't live looking backward. More often than not, I'm far more excited about what's ahead of me. I often feel this overwhelming sense that something good is coming for me. Something amazing. That said, I'll probably remember the first talisman I ever made for the rest of my life.

In prison, a "shakedown" is when anywhere from two to ten guards come to your cell and turn your whole world into a broken jumble on the floor. Sometimes there is a side dish of physical brutality if you're one of the few they pick out to rough up that day. When I was incarcerated, a shakedown would happen an average of once a month. It was a source of constant stress and anxiety, a kind of psychological torture. It was during one of these shakedowns that I made my first talisman.

I could see the guards making their way down the tier. I knew it was going to take them at least an hour to get to me. I sat on my bunk and picked up my coffee cup and a pen. I turned the coffee cup upside down on a piece of white paper and traced around the lip of it in order to make a perfect circle. Once I had the circle, I flipped open Donald Michael Kraig's *Modern Magick*. In it was a lesson on all different ways to create a talisman. The method that piqued my interest the most was one employed by the Hermetic Order of the Golden Dawn. To do it, you used an illustration they had created of a rose. Each petal of the rose held a letter of the alphabet. You drew a line from letter to letter of the word you were spelling, until you end up with a sigil, a squiggly line that represents the word. I chose the word "protection." I used this Rose Cross diagram to draw this squiggly line in the center of the circle I'd drawn using the coffee cup. And then, just because I still had some time before they got to me, and I wanted to use it to put as much energy into creating the talisman as possible, I began writing "protect me from all guards" around the edge of the circle in a coded magickal alphabet.

I chose to charge the talisman with the energy of the element of fire. I hadn't started my nonstop daily angel invocations yet—they still smacked too much of Christianity to me, and I had too many childhood memories of fundamentalists. At that time, I worked almost exclusively with elemental energy. There was nothing religious to my mind about earth, air, fire, and water.

I focused my attention on the energy center in the center of my chest, doing the charging practices you have been reading about. Once I felt like the energy and my concentration had peaked, I released all of the chi to flow from the heart center down my arms, out of my hands, and into the talisman. As the light saturated the talisman, I saw it in my mind as being filled with intense red light, since red is the color of fire. I had time to go through this process twice more before the guards got to my cell, and I tried to put as much energy as possible into it. You could actually do this hundreds of times, creating an incredibly powerful artifact, if you had the time and inclination to do so.

When I finished, I closed the talisman up inside the book I'd been using and left it lying on the concrete slab that served as a bed. When the guards came into my cell, there were five of them—a sergeant and four underlings. The underlings all waited for a cue from the sergeant to see how much damage he wanted them to do. The sergeant sat down on my bunk and began looking through a copy of *GQ* magazine someone had sent me. "I saw y'all on the news again the other day," he said to me. "Folks are saying y'all are going to get out soon. That true?"

I honestly didn't know which answer he wanted to hear, yes or no. "From your mouth to God's ear," was what I finally said to him.

"I hope you sue these motherfuckers for millions," he said. Then he stood up and nodded for the underlings to get out. They all left without touching a single thing.

After that, I used sigils and talismans a lot. Eventually I'd end up having them tattooed over large parts of my body, so that I could wear them as a permanent shield.

ROSE CROSS
SIGIL CREATOR

Sigils are potent talismans and magickal batteries that can also help in visualizing because they eliminate the need for intricate, detailed visualizations of people, places, or things. A sigil is a tool that holds the energy you put into it, so you don't have to continually think or visualize whatever outcome you're working toward. The sigil on the cover of this book represents magick.

A sigil is a shape that acts as an actual physical representation of whatever thing or condition you want to manifest, or the energy you wish to use to manifest it. Sigils are effective because they let you work in all levels of reality to attain your desired result. I have written much about sigils in my books *High Magick* and *Angels & Archangels*, but I have never shared instructions on how to make one yourself until now.

To create a sigil, choose a word like the name of an element, planet, or angel that represents the energy you wish to generate, or something that represents your desired outcome.

Place a piece of paper over the Rose Cross template on page 192.

The sigil starts with a circle and ends with a line. Find the first letter of your word. Draw a small circle there.

Starting from the small circle, use a straightedge to connect each letter of the word from the center of one "petal" to the next. When you get to the last letter draw a short line perpendicular to the line you just drew, right where it ends.

If a letter does not exist on the template, then use the sound of the letter instead, or if that is not possible then omit the letter completely from the sigil.

You can draw this sigil on any object or simply on a piece of paper. You can charge it with the energy of an element, angel, or any other beneficial force.

See Page 234 for charts of elemental correspondences.

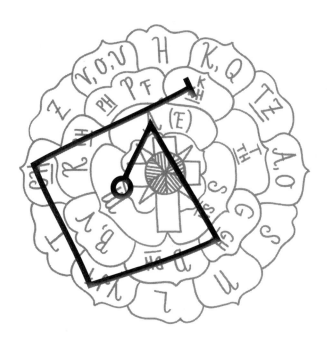

PART 6

MANIFESTATION
& MASTERY

One of my students asked me recently what I think about the Law of Attraction. I replied that it is basically watered-down magick. There is nothing wrong with attracting beneficial things and experiences into your life, but once you have them, what then? The Law of Attraction teachings are not a complete path. Will acquiring another six Rolls-Royces bring you liberation or serve to awaken you to the truth of who you are? As I have said before, I see magick as the Western equivalent of the Eastern traditions that have a goal of freedom from the cycle of existence. That said, even those traditions teach that it is fine to experience a prosperous life, particularly if you don't get hung up on the material world as the be-all and end-all of existence. The physical world is just one level of reality—more about that a little later in this section.

I was having dinner at my favorite restaurant in Harlem one night. I told our friends that I would pay the check if they'd do magick with me. They agreed. When the check came, it was $140. I asked them to do magick, in whatever their preferred way was, for that $140 to return to me tenfold. We then spent about two minutes sitting around the table with our eyes closed, charging the check as a talisman.

Less than a month later a publisher in another country who wanted to buy translation rights to one of my books contacted me. They were offering $1,400.

Another example is my tours of the Met. I had spent a straight month doing hours of ritual work with the focus of having an amazing job in a rich, beautiful environment that I loved, something that would contribute to my completion of the Great Work, something that made me happy. Almost by accident and with no pre-thought, I found myself conducting tours at the Metropolitan Museum of Art in Manhattan. I just woke up one day and announced on social media that "as of today I will be conducting tours of the Met." Suddenly every time I looked at the calendar, another tour had been booked. The Met became my office and second home. I worked in a place more rich and priceless than any of the offices of the biggest companies in New York. Sometimes I would look around me and think, "This is where you work. You get to spend every day in this epicenter of beauty and magick, a virtual 3D map of the aeons."

Actually, it all was set in motion when I was with one of the two guys I did magick with at the restaurant. He told me, "If you want fine things in your life, then you should go to places where you'll be surrounded by fine things." From then on, I put a great deal of thought into everywhere I went. I never really went into bars after that because they weren't part of a life I wanted. And I started spending as much time as possible surrounded by depth, history, and beauty.

I started spending time at the Metropolitan Museum of Art, which holds some of the most priceless and magickal objects on earth. Exploring New York with a new sense of discovery, I visited cathedrals, museums, and places that held the energy of devotion and love of Divinity; places designed to retrain your mind to focus on things above the mundane and mediocre.

Every building starts with a drawn plan with words called "specs" that describe how to construct it.

Everything we see in the physical world began with a thought, or a collection of thoughts.

The mind is the starting point and the connecting link to the manifest and unmanifest worlds.

Nothing can stand between you and the dreams that you choose mentally, and then project outwardly through your spoken and written words or imagination.

THOUGHTS
& WORDS

I started to examine and take seriously my thought life about five years ago. In the beginning my mind was so wrought with fear, judgment, and just a general sloppy mess of words like "can't," "won't," "hate," words carrying so much negative weight it was no wonder I found myself sinking into the mire of mediocrity and lack.

Just starting small with changing your thoughts will bring about huge results. Some of the things I suggest may make you think: "That won't change anything, it's just a thought." Well, just try even one of these exercises on a daily basis and see how differently you start to feel.

First thing in the morning upon awakening, think of joy flooding your heart, and envision gold light filling up your chest, your body, and then illuminating your whole room. The thought of joy will change the course of your morning. You can add an angelic or divine presence to this practice, as in the "Upon Waking" ritual, if you wish, but you can also keep it very simple.

When you look in the mirror, say out loud, or think to yourself: "You're beautiful! I love you so dearly." Again, it sounds corny, but if you say it, or think it about yourself, it will eventually open you up to healing long-standing wounds you've inflicted upon *yourself*. Feelings of "I'm not deserving of a full, rich life" or "I'm not good enough." If you're tough on yourself (like I am), thoughts and words of love afford a little softness and tenderness to take root. It also helps you find love for others more easily. If you love and forgive yourself, it's a great start in loving and forgiving others.

As the day progresses, when you see people,
try to see and think of a golden spark in them,
as I suggested in Part 3. As you pass them
on the street or in the workplace, or even in
the people with whom you live, envision that
spark of gold. It helps to see all people as
sharing that one energy source. Even if we or
they may not be acting like it, it's still there.

At the end of the day, look at all you've done
and bless all your relationships, projects, and
interactions with divine love. Just think or
say to yourself, "I bless this situation with
divine love," and see how it feels. During sleep,
your subconscious mind will let go of the
problems or snags, and divine love will start
to work in ways you'll never quite believe.

I now find I can be aware of my thoughts maybe 50 percent of the time. I'm able to see a thought come into my mind and have the buffer to decide: should I say this out loud or not? Most of the time, I decide the thought need not be uttered.

I've become much more conscious of my idle chatter and my judgments about myself or others. It's taken a long time, and the work will never be finished, but I think I'm better for being a little bit quieter.

I think Damien thinks so, too. But, being the quiet type, he hasn't used his words to say it!

MANIFESTATION
101

Your thoughts and words are the basics, it's true. From the mind come words that elaborate on the images the mind creates, which is why it's extremely important to mind what you say. Speak words of gratitude, love, and positivity.

There are other ways to imprint your desires upon the energetic levels of reality as well:

Writing down your dreams or drawing pictures of what you desire are amazing aids in manifesting.

Looking at images of actual physical representations of things you want to bring into your life can also help. For instance, if you want a new house, spend time searching for images online, then create a folder, page, or document where you can save those photos and look at them so that they become embedded in your imagination.

You can add some energy to these basic manifestation practices by using a charging ritual to infuse them with your intention and/or call upon the assistance of an element, planet, or angel.

CHILD MIND

This morning, as I made coffee for Damien and myself, I thought of how my mind worked as a child. I've realized that the soul of me has never changed. What I mean is that the pure essence of who I am, without the trappings of ego, has never changed. This is why the pure joy I felt as a child still feels the same as it does now.

We create as children in a way that we tend to forget as we grow older. The worries and responsibilities pile on top of what we are, what we are meant to be: that which creates, that which God manifests this creation through.

I've heard it said that when we are born, our souls are connected to God and the earth like a straw, and God's love moves through us with ease; that is the child's wonder at everything, the pure giddiness and joy. Eventually that straw gets mucked up with worry, guilt, judgment, and anger until our connection to God is cut off, sometimes completely. Our memory of what it's like to live as a spiritual creature creating a material world is forgotten.

As I poured coffee and fed the cats and fish, memories of childhood flooded back to me, and I realized how many things I thought of as a child had actually manifested. I laughed as I remembered dreaming of a boy from space who would land on earth. In my tiny single bed before I fell asleep, I would envision taking him around the world, introducing him to different foods and my favorite places.

Yeah. That's what I got.

As a twelve-year-old, I was bound and determined to live in New York, work in a fancy building, go see any movie I wanted to see. I'd sit on our front porch, reading the film reviews in the *New Yorker*, and in my mind, I was in the theaters, seeing the films. Later I did exactly that; I worked in one of the most beautiful buildings in Soho and saw every single movie I had read about all those years ago.

This morning, sitting in bed, sipping our coffees, I asked Damien if he remembered any of his childhood dreams and whether or not they had come to pass.

His answer was brilliant. Being born with dark brown hair, he longed for the jet-black color of his parent's hair. I looked closely: not even a trace of brown, and he's never been near hair dye (except for the time he got some silver streaks).

He then said the first time he saw Bruce Willis he thought his receding hairline was exceedingly handsome and wished it for himself. As a child of eight or so, to wish upon yourself a receding hairline is so . . . well, so very Damien. Have a look at a photo of him sometime.

As I continue to do spiritual work, I'm feeling lighter, and more childlike. I find more joy and giddiness, a moving away from the judgment that has had me mired in the mundane for years and years. We're all so careless with ourselves, allowing hate to overtake us, even when we don't understand that it's happening. It starts very, very early. Think back to when we first start casting blame, or attacking because someone has taken what we deem as ours, or talking about the kids who are different from us, or bullying others. It starts when we are young, and charts a corrosive, destructive path that leads to broken lives, pain, and fear.

There's always time to put it all right again. The shift can come in an instant, the moment we decide to change our thoughts, watch what we say, and stay at it until we cleanse that conduit that connects us to God.

SLEEP
MANIFESTATION
MAGICK

As you prepare for sleep, speak to yourself about what you are:

"I am creative. I am confident. I am
talented. I am prosperous. I am willing.
I am open to potential. My life is divinely
orchestrated and perfectly successful."

Whatever it is that you are doing magick for, speak it
and prepare your mind to receive it as you're going to
sleep. Your mind will take these statements as the truth,
and will, over time, begin to manifest those things.

LASSOING
TIME

I'm a procrastinator.

During my university years studying landscape architecture, I was the one in the studio for seventy-two hours straight, sleep deprived, my mind warped into a new reality, working to complete the project I'd had four weeks to complete.

In my adult life I worked in offices. The strict confines of nine-to-five helped in mediating my delaying tactics—I couldn't watch a movie, or read a book, or whip up scrambled eggs while at my desk, so I got my work in on time. I found structure was needed in my life; it gave me balance and evened out the anxiety us dilly-dalliers experience every second of every waking hour.

My life and work changed abruptly after Damien's release from prison. No longer was I working for a firm; I was flung into being a movie producer, a public speaker, a writer, and an artist.

While I relished in the freedom and joy of creativity, I was back to a structureless existence.

Projects now hung in the ether waiting for me to address them, like silent wallflowers hoping for the chance to dance.

Anxiety became a familiar shroud as I would begin every day with: "Today I'll start writing that book" or "Today I'll begin the drawings for that art show."

The days filed by, one after another, as I whittled time away like an old man with a pocketknife and a stick.

The Quakers have a saying, "Pray, and move your feet." It is important to match your thoughts and words with actions if you are to see change in your life.

Talking with a friend of mine who has a similar affliction, she offered a solution, an app that times your activities. You sit down, start the timer, and work for twenty-five minutes. After that amount of time, a small chime sounds and you take a five-minute break. This break can't be checking emails or looking at social media; you must get up and do something.

I was desperate. Having gotten the app, I sat down with my laptop, typed in the task I was about to dive into—"BOOK"—and set to work.

I nearly jumped when the chime snapped me out of my concentration. I got up, did some jumping jacks, made a tea, played with the cats, and the chime called me back.

My friend calls it the "Benevolent Taskmaster." If you don't have an app, use a common kitchen timer or the alarm on your phone.

People often speak of writers as being ritualistic. I couldn't claim that attribute before, but now not only is lassoing time in small batches a Godsend, it has become one of my favorite daily rituals.

HEALING LACK
WITH ANGEL
MAGICK

I was raised in an environment that was immersed in a poverty mentality. My father grew up poor, the kind of poor that most can never understand. It's the stuff of novels and movies, *Angela's Ashes* or *The Glass Castle*, often looked upon as something that only exists in stories.

My father's mother died in childbirth, leaving him a bereft two-year-old without the benefit of any softness in his world. His was a childhood filled with fear; the monster in the closet that threatened to tear him limb from limb. He had no one to soothe or calm his terrors.

He brought that fear into our family; the stripped-down, sinewy, gnawing monster that now hid in my closet, the unseen terror that I may end up alone, broke, living on the streets with nothing and no one.

The dark shadow of a poverty mentality followed me into adulthood where I would fear getting fired from every job, dread the phone bills that Damien and I would rack up, inevitably, our need for connection trumping my ability to manage the steep premium it cost.

Fast forward to 2019. I made a pact with God.

Having let the locusts feed on my soul for far too long, I was bound to rise above it. If a caterpillar could do it, then so could I. Never being one for New Year's resolutions, it was with surprise that I sat down with a paper and pen to create a memorialized promise that I would no longer fear lack.

For me, this meant giving 10 percent of our income to the place(s) I received inspiration; to the teachers or institutions that enabled me to grow spiritually.

Starting out was scary. There were times I couldn't see a way out—tax bills looming, a visit to the emergency room in an era when insurance was scarce, unexpected bills. And yet, I refused to give in to fear, sometimes waking in the night, the icy, cold threat of lack staring me in the face, and I could only come back to "be still and know that I am God."

My dark time lasted for a long time; nothing was happening. I was doing the work, and yet I wasn't seeing the light. I couldn't see anything changing on the material plane.

What was working in the spiritual realm was something quite different. As each bill or need loomed, there came a saving grace—a job or an opportunity would arise and we'd be okay.

I can now say that hard kernel of fear has been dissolved. I trust God will fulfill our every need and provide far more than I can even imagine—not only in material things, but in the room I have in my heart for love, patience, forgiveness, and joy. Fear eats away all the space, and I'm done with it—its lease is up.

The most surprising aspect of this work, when you finally get on the other side of it, is that you realize whatever it is that requires work becomes your teacher. I can now look lack right in the face and thank it for all it has taught me. It's banished from my soul, and I've sent it on its way, but I bless it, even as I bid it adieu: "Don't let the screen door hit your ass on your way out."

I learned this technique from the magickal author Damon Brand.

When fear of lack arises, call upon an archangel
or other spiritual entity. This can be as simple as
saying their name or bringing them to mind.

Speak with them about the lack you've
endured. Really unburden yourself.

Then speak of what you will do with the
prosperity that will come into your life.

It only takes a minute, but the excitement created in
that tiny fraction of time when you switch over from the
feeling of lack to the feeling of abundance creates great
excitement—and that is where the alchemy comes in. It
is transmutation of one state of being to another, a tiny
explosion of energy.

THANKS IN
ADVANCE

The most important ritual we can do is to constantly surrender to God.

We all want things. Being human, we come into this world wanting—a warm bed, nourishing food, a loving presence to take care of us.

Later on, there are toys, kittens, bikes, and candy. We want so many delicious, comforting, exciting things. As we grow older, we begin to believe that if we don't get our coveted wishes, we simply won't be happy, safe, complete, or loved.

The ego takes over, clambering for that situation, person, job, and it makes us crazy, thinking that if we don't get it, we will never be fulfilled. We will be incomplete.

Wanting things isn't a bad thing. Once we learn what we're here to do, the wanting seems to fade away into being, which is hard to understand, but we eventually know that we are already complete.

The only problem with wanting is, if we latch on and wait, wait, wait for it to manifest, then what we're focusing on is that fact that we don't *have* it. We're focusing on lack, and lack will perpetuate.

As much as I am loathe to expose my lack of spiritual prowess, here's a little story about something I wanted and how I managed to get everything wrong.

I needed some advice, so I reached out to a few people I knew could send me in the right direction. I sent out some emails and waited to hear back, fully expecting to have a plethora of information from which I could plan for a huge step in my work.

At first I thought, "Oh, it's the holidays, I'll hear back soon after." But nothing came, nary a bite. I began checking my email every five minutes, refreshing my phone and laptop. I'd check junk mail. Radio silence.

I went into full-on spin mode. I was convinced magick didn't work, that I would never get the information I needed, meaning the project I want more than anything would never, ever come to pass. Damien watched as I had a full-on meltdown on our living room floor.

I gave up. I simply gave up. But it wasn't an enlightened surrender, it was a childish, throwing-hands-in-the-air quitting.

Then, from my place on the floor, I heard Damien say: "Your phone is ringing." I jumped up. It was one of the very kind people I had contacted calling to help me.

The miracle came when I gave up my expectations—even poorly. God doesn't care how you hand over the reins, as long as you do.

Damien, who doesn't make me feel bad when I act like an idiot (sweet man), told me that I needed to let go. Really let go.

So, I'm doing my best. And things really are getting better. A few wonderful surprises have happened since, but the most extraordinary thing is I feel at peace.

I now have a new ritual for those moments when I question creation. I whisper aloud:

Thank you for answering my prayers.

That's all. No "please answer my prayers, in this way, at this time, with this person." In those moments of peace and clarity, there is room where God can fill me up.

THE PATH
OF MAGICK

Technically speaking, there's nothing "sacred" or "holy" about magick. When we're speaking of any aspect of ceremonial magick—from attaining enlightenment, to freeing yourself from the endless cycle of incarnating into the physical world, to something like manifesting a new career or a suitable companion—what we're doing is using a science. It's a "spiritual science"—meaning one that's not understood by the world at large yet—but a science nonetheless. The job of a magician is to understand how these things work in a way that is stripped of superstition and mysticism, in order to make use of it all in concrete, practical ways.

A big part of being a magician is knowing how magick works . . . and in order to understand that, we have to understand a little more about how we—and the universe—are structured. When you understand the structure and mechanics of the metaphysical aspects of the universe (and by extension your own soul), you will also understand the way magick manifests in the physical world and be a much more proficient magician.

"As above, so below." This is one of the most well-known axioms in all of magick. It means, in part, that whatever is happening in the external world is simply a reflection of an energetic occurrence on the more subtle, or energetic, planes of reality. It also means that whatever processes are taking place in the universe around us are also happening on a much smaller scale within each and every one of us. This means that every single person on earth is a tiny, miniature universe unto themselves. To understand what this means, it's necessary to understand that the nature of reality is much, much bigger than what we can perceive with our physical senses. In fact, all that we perceive around us is just one single level of reality: the physical plane. In addition to the physical plane, there are four other "higher," or more subtle, planes. In fact, when we do magick, it is on these higher planes where the work occurs. The magick we do then manifests into the physical realm as it descends down through the levels of creation.

There are different kinds of magick that can be done to have an effect on each of these levels. For example, when we are doing elemental work—anything from invoking the archangels of the four elements to charging a candle or talisman with the energy of one of the elements—we are working with the etheric level of reality. The etheric level is made up of the densest kind of energy, which is known in certain Eastern internal alchemical traditions as "chi."

When we work with planetary energies—anything from invoking the archangel of a specific planet to obtain its aid and blessing, to charging crystals or herbs with planetary energy (for example, the energy of Jupiter for prosperity)—we are working with astral energy. Astral energy is more subtle and ethereal than etheric energy because it is from a higher plane.

When we're working with any of the energies that correspond to the spheres on the Tree of Life of the Kabbalah teachings, we're working with an energy that's even more ethereal than that of the astral plane. It's known as the energy of the mental plane. This is the plane in which abstract concepts reside.

And lastly, the highest level of reality of all is the spiritual plane, or spiritual level, of reality. This is the level from which everything in existence was born and to which all will one day return. The spiritual level of reality is beyond the comprehension of the intellect entirely.

Here are the levels of reality and how we do magick with them, from the densest to the most ethereal:

- **THE PHYSICAL:** which we bring into play by utilizing the physical world in our rituals— such as burning a candle or performing certain gestures such as mudras

- **THE ETHERIC**: which we access when we do elemental magick

- **THE ASTRAL**: which we access when we do planetary magick

- **THE MENTAL**: which we access when we do magick involving the spheres on the Tree of Life

- **AND THE SPIRITUAL**: which can usually only be accessed by individuals who have been doing this work for years and have reached the stages of development we'd call either being an adept or a master

These levels of reality exist not only externally, but also internally, as layers of the aura. There is an etheric layer of the aura, an astral layer of the aura, a mental layer of the aura, and a spiritual layer of the aura. The level of our energy system that corresponds to the physical level of reality is our body—which is the densest and most concrete level of our anatomy. We begin the path seeking to fulfill our needs on the physical level. If we complete the Great Work, we master every level of reality and remain masters of ourselves, even in death.

In magick there are traditionally three levels of development a mage passes through on their way towards completion of the Great Work: neophyte, adept, and master. I offer you this blessing as neophytes on the path.

May the power, blessings, and favor of Raphael, archangel and guardian of the East and ruler of the element of air, descend upon you in order to protect, guide, and illuminate you on your journey through life and on the path of High Magick.

May the power, blessings, and favor of Michael, archangel and guardian of the South and ruler of the element of fire, descend upon you in order to protect, guide, and illuminate you on your journey through life and on the path of High Magick.

May the power, blessings, and favor of Gabriel, archangel and guardian of the West and ruler of the element of water, descend upon you in order to protect, guide, and illuminate you on your journey through life and on the path of High Magick.

May the power, blessings, and favor of Uriel, archangel and guardian of the North and ruler of the element of earth, descend upon you in order to protect, guide, and illuminate you on your journey through life and on the path of High Magick.

EPILOGUE

DOING WORK IN DEEP WATERS

Have you ever wanted something so badly—a dream that's been put in your heart, a circumstance you have longed for—yet it doesn't manifest? It's "stuck," unmoving, or so you feel it is.

The year 2004 was a dark time. I had been living in Little Rock for five years after learning about Damien's case in 1996. We married in 1999. We had momentum; the worldwide cause to free the innocent "West Memphis Three" had brought in some serious money and support, but as legal cases often go, we were at a standstill. The lawyers had filed their briefs, and the courts simply made no reply.

Keeping hope alive under those dire circumstances was like forever scanning the hard blue skies for a scant, small patch of cloud, even as you watch the crops turn to dust. The months turned into years. From 2003 to 2007 we had run amok in a bleak no-man's-land, our

provisions dwindling. The delirious love and desire we had for each other was in danger of being trampled by the abject horror we encountered every single day.

Somewhere in the depths of that hell, a friend gave me a copy of the I Ching. I threw the coins and read:

> The **future** is embodied in **Hexagram 5— (Waiting)**: With sincerity, there will be brilliant success. With firmness there will be good fortune, and it will be advantageous to cross the great stream.

It's all I had to cling to, and I grabbed on. Each morning I threw the coins and read. It was such a small thing, but the words filled up my starving soul, and I could slowly feel myself come back to life.

Next, I began a sitting meditation. Upon getting out of bed, I would sit on the floor quietly for seven minutes, trying to think only of cleaning my spirit, my energy. It was a simple, basic ritual, but it was changing me, minute by minute. I was getting stronger, more alive, and as I healed, so did my relationship with Damien, for he had begun his own methods of magick by then.

We didn't know it at the time, but we were still four years out from his release. Looking back, I'm certain if we hadn't experienced such pain and pulled ourselves kicking and screaming through the muck, we wouldn't have had the strength to endure the massive changes that were in our future.

Another word for magick is prayer, and I tend to use that word; it's what I grew up with. In my own life, I've

seen prayers answered in the most remarkable ways, and I'm grateful each and every time a prayer is manifested. But I've found the hardest things to bring about are the things that are at the very core of our life's work. Maybe it's over-coming a poverty mentality or a sense of powerlessness; maybe it's to realize unconditional love or to escape being a victim. The very thing that is entrenched in your soul, the very thing you feel holds you back from your life of abun-dance is the thing you must overcome.

So much fear is associated with the unknown, the depths of the dark water, but that's just looking at things on the surface. The absolute certainty of it is that there *are* extremely spooky things down there, but there are also treasures and mysteries, and what could be better than that?

The ocean floor is thirty-six thousand feet at its deepest; that's seven thousand feet more than the height of Everest. Down there, in a world that scientists are still discovering, live the scariest of fish: creatures that actually electrocute their prey, and others that don't bother with any prepara-tions, they just swallow the living whole.

There's beauty, though, in the fish that create their own light source. Like hundreds of lightning bugs moving silently through their dark, velvety world. It's called bioluminescence, and it's nothing short of magickal, creating bright stars in a black, inky sky.

There's also sunken treasure. Three years ago, a Spanish ship was discovered that contained a fortune worth sev-enteen billion. Strange worlds remain down there—whole pyramids, huge limestone roadways, and the remnants of entire cities remain etched into the sandy landscape.

So, if given the choice, where would you rather be? In bright shallows, or in the deep waters, where the mystical merges with the terrifying and the unknown abundance is as bountiful as the number of stars in the sky?

Imagine you're way out there, floating on the surface of calm blue. The sun shines, the wind blows a cool breeze, and you know there are mysteries in every direction. Be excited about the hugeness of it and give it all to God and relax, float for a few moments.

Do work in the deep waters.

JOY IN EVERY MOMENT

Back when Lorri first found me, we wrote letters that were full of detailed descriptions about the life we would create together in the free world.

We wrote of traveling the world, having the freedom to do whatever creative work we wanted to do, and we envisioned even the most mundane of experiences as magickal, that our days would be filled with joy.

Magick enriched my life and protected me while I was on death row. My release plunged me into a complex trauma even I couldn't understand. Those around me weren't capable of seeing the damage, and most of it was interior wounds that couldn't be seen.

Traveling the world instantly manifested, having two books and a film to promote in the first two years of my freedom. By the start of my third year out, I had suffered my second nervous breakdown.

I wasn't capable of managing my life at that time, let alone my magick practice. Eventually Lorri and I hit rock bottom, and we found we weren't functioning as a couple and barely as humans.

We initiated a slow but steady routine of building rituals into our lives, some of which are included in this book. We spent whole days in separate rooms, each of us building our spiritual practice so that we could build a foundation for a new life together.

It took time and patience and the faith that God would heal us, not only restore us, but bring us out stronger, better.

I'm so happy to report that we persevered and now have a relationship that's thriving. I've never been happier, and our home is filled with joy and love. We can finally say that the biggest manifestation of all has come. Joy in every moment; in the mundane, and in the extraordinary.

ACKNOWLEDGMENTS

Damien and Lorri would like to thank everyone at Sounds True, especially Tami Simon, Jennifer Brown, Jade Lascelles, Jeff Mack, and Kriste Peoples, for without them this book wouldn't exist. To Henry Dunow—truly the best agent and a huge support.

To our fellow magicians: John Michael Greer, Michelle Belanger, Ricardo Villanova, Derek Dunaven, Pablo Mercado, Asma Rul, Mayela Gutierrez, Ilona Virostek, David Reyes, Seane Corn, and Jay Conner, thank you for all the wisdom.

To Sherry Chico for being the best sister and teacher. All our love . . .

Thank you, Rohini Walker and Terry Taylor-Castillo, Martin Mancha, and everyone at The Joshua Tree Retreat Center for the most inspiring place to teach.

Thank you, Kate Cazee, Crystal Nye, and Ruth Carter for seeing us through the pandemic. We didn't have to go a single day without toilet paper or hand sanitizer!

To all of our amazing friends to whom we're eternally grateful, especially Philippa Boyens, Fran Walsh and Peter

Jackson, Tracy McCort, Shelley Huber, Deborah Strefella, Josh Wakely, Zach Hunter, Kevin Wilson, Matthew Goldman, Matt Fennell, Jeremy Fridell, Mare Hieronimus, and Steve Braga.

Thank you to our families and all the wonderful people who have supported us on Patreon, many of whom feel like family.

Thank you to our new home city, New Orleans (Anastasia); you have taken us in with open arms, and for that we love you.

APPENDIX

ELEMENTAL CORRESPONDENCES

ELEMENT	TIME	QUALITY	POLARITY	COLOR
Air	Dawn	Warm & Moist	Masculine	Yellow
Fire	Noon	Warm & Dry	Masculine	Red
Water	Sunset	Cool & Moist	Feminine	Blue & White
Earth	Night	Cool & Dry	Feminine	Green & Brown

DIRECTION	SEASON	DOMAIN	ASTROLOGICAL SIGNS
East	Spring	Breath & Communication	Aquarius, Gemini, Libra
South	Summer	Passions & Lifeforce	Sagittarius, Aries, Leo
West	Autumn	Maturity of Emotions & Subconscious	Cancer, Scorpio, Pisces
North	Winter	Physical Body & Material Things	Capricorn, Taurus, Virgo

ELEMENTAL CORRESPONDENCES CONT.

ELEMENT	METAL	GEMSTONE & MINERAL	TAROT SUIT
Air	Mercury	Malachite, Jade	Swords
Fire	Gold	Ruby, Carnelian	Wands
Water	Silver	Lapis Lazuli, Moonstone	Cups
Earth	Lead	Salt	Pentacles

PLANTS & AROMATICS	MAGICKAL TOOL	ARCHANGEL
Bergamot, Sandalwood	Athame/ Dagger	Raphael
Cinnamon, Cloves, Copal, Rosemary	Wand	Michael
Rose, Ylang Ylang	Chalice	Gabriel
Comfrey, Vervain, Patchouli	Pentacle	Uriel

PLANETARY CORRESPONDENCES

PLANET	ELEMENT	COLOR	DAY	NUMBER
Saturn	Earth	Black	Saturday	3
Jupiter	Fire	Blue	Thursday	4
Mars	Fire	Red	Tuesday	5
Sun	Fire	Gold	Sunday	6
Venus	Water	Green	Friday	7
Mercury	Air	Orange	Wednesday	8
Moon	Water	Purple	Monday	9

METAL	STONE	EDIBLE HERB	INCENSE	ARCHANGEL
Lead	Black Onyx, Jet	Solomon's Seal Root	Myrrh	Cassiel
Tin	Sapphire, Amethyst	Dandelion	Clove	Sachiel
Iron, Steel	Ruby, Garnet	Blessed Thistle	Dragon's Blood	Zamael
Gold	Tiger's Eye, Citrine	St. John's Wort	Frankincense	Michael
Copper, Bronze	Emerald, Jade	Rose	Rose	Anael
Aluminum, Mercury	Carnelian	Lavender	Bergamot	Raphael
Silver	Moonstone, Alexandrite	Blue Lotus	Ylang Ylang	Gabriel

ABOUT
THE AUTHORS

Lorri Davis and Damien Echols live in New Orleans with their two cats, where they practice Magick, devoting themselves to the Great Work. There may also be some strolls through the Xanadu that is the French Quarter.

To learn more about their work, visit patreon.com, where both Lorri and Damien publish original content. To learn more about their story, see the documentary *West of Memphis* or go to damienechols.com.

ABOUT
SOUNDS TRUE

Sounds True is a multimedia publisher whose mission is to inspire and support personal transformation and spiritual awakening. Founded in 1985 and located in Boulder, Colorado, we work with many of the leading spiritual teachers, thinkers, healers, and visionary artists of our time. We strive with every title to preserve the essential "living wisdom" of the author or artist. It is our goal to create products that not only provide information to a reader or listener but also embody the quality of a wisdom transmission.

For those seeking genuine transformation, Sounds True is your trusted partner. At SoundsTrue.com you will find a wealth of free resources to support your journey, including exclusive weekly audio interviews, free downloads, interactive learning tools, and other special savings on all our titles.

To learn more, please visit
SoundsTrue.com/freegifts
or call us toll-free at 800.333.9185